D0097976

THE
SILENT
SALESMEN

THE
SILENT
SALESMEN

Guaranteed Strategies for Increasing Sales and Profits Using Promotional Products

MITCH CARSON

WILEY

John Wiley & Sons, Inc.

Copyright © 2009 by Mitch Carson. All rights reserved.

Published by John Wiley & Sons, Inc., Hoboken, New Jersey.
Published simultaneously in Canada.

No part of this publication may be reproduced, stored in a retrieval system, or transmitted in any form or by any means, electronic, mechanical, photocopying, recording, scanning, or otherwise, except as permitted under Section 107 or 108 of the 1976 United States Copyright Act, without either the prior written permission of the Publisher, or authorization through payment of the appropriate per-copy fee to the Copyright Clearance Center, Inc., 222 Rosewood Drive, Danvers, MA 01923, (978) 750-8400, fax (978) 646-8600, or on the web at www.copyright.com. Requests to the Publisher for permission should be addressed to the Permissions Department, John Wiley & Sons, Inc., 111 River Street, Hoboken, NJ 07030, (201) 748-6011, fax (201) 748-6008, or online at http://www.wiley.com/go/permissions.

Limit of Liability/Disclaimer of Warranty: While the publisher and author have used their best efforts in preparing this book, they make no representations or warranties with respect to the accuracy or completeness of the contents of this book and specifically disclaim any implied warranties of merchantability or fitness for a particular purpose. No warranty may be created or extended by sales representatives or written sales materials. The advice and strategies contained herein may not be suitable for your situation. You should consult with a professional where appropriate. Neither the publisher nor author shall be liable for any loss of profit or any other commercial damages, including but not limited to special, incidental, consequential, or other damages.

For general information on our other products and services or for technical support, please contact our Customer Care Department within the United States at (800) 762-2974, outside the United States at (317) 572-3993 or fax (317) 572-4002.

Wiley also publishes its books in a variety of electronic formats. Some content that appears in print may not be available in electronic books. For more information about Wiley products, visit our web site at www.wiley.com.

Library of Congress Cataloging-in-Publication Data:

Carson, Mitch, 1960-
  The silent salesmen : guaranteed strategies for increasing sales and profits using promotional products / Mitch Carson.
      p. cm.
  Includes bibliographical references and index.
  ISBN 978-0-470-27035-6 (cloth)
1. Sales promotion.   2. Marketing.   I. Title.
  HF5438.5.C37 2008
  658.8'2–dc22   2008033887

ISBN-13: 978-0-470-27035-6

Printed in the United States of America.

10 9 8 7 6 5 4 3 2 1

To my late mother, Geraldine Carson: You always said I could do and be whatever I wanted. Well, mom, your son is finally a published author.

CONTENTS

FOREWORD

Eight years ago on a hot autumn day in Phoenix, Arizona, I met Mitch Carson for the first time. He was sitting with a business partner in a restaurant and because I was by myself, he took note and used an open palm gesture to point out the empty chair. Without having said a word, I understood what Mitch meant and grabbed a seat at his table. We began talking, quickly found we had a lot in common, and eventually became good friends.

Over the course of the next hour, Mitch and I spoke about many subjects—but we always came back to two of our favorites: martial arts and marketing.

Although Mitch never made mention of his illustrious background as a karate fighting champion, I was well aware that I was sitting next to someone with great skill; someone who didn't need to blow his horn. His skills were written all over his face and body. You could see the discipline in his posture, the focus in his eyes, and the determination carved into the marrow of his bones.

Perhaps of even greater importance, when speaking to Mitch I knew I was dealing with someone who didn't need to put on airs. I knew I was talking to someone who was giving me the straight scoop. There's something about a human being who trains his mind and body for years, then enters the ring and emerges victorious time and again. In Mitch's case, it's the quiet, calming confidence of a champion. Anyone who has won nearly 300 grand championships has developed his internal power to the point that his external world will reflect it.

And this leads to my most important point about Mitch: Champion athletes and martial artists, at the highest levels of accomplishment, are often also extraordinary entrepreneurs. They already know about having goals, being focused, and adding energy to your every action. They know how to deliver a punch that improves sales. They know how to throw lightning fast, nearly invisible combinations of punches and kicks that knock doors down and get people to take action. They know when to hit hard—when to hit softly—and when to walk away.

I've watched Mitch take failing businesses and punch up their sales with *The Silent Salesmen* approach to marketing. I've seen him take businesses that were already doing well and explode their profits. And I've watched him calmly walk onto a stage and stand before large groups of men and women who didn't want to spend a dime on another product or service. An hour later, these same people clamored around Mitch begging him to take their money. Not a single person in the room felt "sold." Every single person who bought from him, believed deep down in his gut that Mitch was helping him or her go to the next level in business.

That he was.

The truth is there are hundreds of riveting stories I could tell you about Mitch Carson and what he has done for so many—but there are two things I want to leave you with that will give you deep insight into the soul and character of this fine man.

The first is the phrase: "I'm going to get good at this." I'll never forget the day that Mitch began his radio show in Los Angeles. To put it mildly, Mitch's first show was not the best I've ever heard. In fact, you might say it flat out stunk. Afterward though, Mitch was not discouraged. He realized he had a lot of improvements to make and he was determined to do whatever it takes to get good.

"I became a champion in karate by making mistakes and correcting them," said Mitch. "I'll do the same with radio."

That he did. Today, Mitch interviews people from all over the world on his show, and I've never heard of a single guest being disappointed.

The second take-away phrase I learned from Mitch was: "No one is going to give more than me."

The first time I heard Mitch say this I was taken aback. Instead of hearing him say he was going to make more money than anyone else, he was saying he was going to give more than others.

You might think this idea antithetical to running a great business, but Mitch has proven time and again that giving is not just good, it's great.

When you give to your prospects and customers, you send *The Silent Salesmen* into their subconscious minds. Everything you give—and much more—comes back to you.

In *The Silent Salesmen*, Mitch Carson gives you more than anyone will ever give you on this subject. Follow his advice and your business profits will soar.

MATT FUREY
www.mattfurey.com

PREFACE

Congratulations! You are on the verge of discovering the astounding power of promotional products. For those of you new to this exciting marketing tool, promotional products are generally useful, and often decorative, items imprinted with a company's name, logo, or message and used in marketing and communications programs. The ultimate intent is to generate more revenue for the company handing out the promotional gifts by giving potential customers something to remember the company by. Though use of promotional products may seem like a simple marketing solution today, the industry itself had a somewhat staggered start.

Let's take a look at one of the first recorded uses of promotional products. Research shows that in 1789, when George Washington was elected president, commemorative buttons were distributed to the public during the election. Wooden specialties, the Farmers' Almanac, and advertising calendars can all be traced back to the early 1800s. However, it wasn't until the latter part of the nineteenth century that a large quantity of promotional products were marketed, helping to create the industry as it is known today.

Making Promotional Products Work for You

You may be wondering how this form of advertising can work for your company. Whether you are looking for a way to motivate your staff, generate more business, encourage customer referrals, increase trade show traffic, introduce a new product, or support your community, promotional products are the answer. Promotional products are used in several ways. Corporate CEOs award employees with desktop accessories or apparel, glassware items or technology toys with logos engraved, screenprinted, or embroidered as an incentive to continue working hard. Marketing departments design products with company names and logos on them and give them away at VIP openings or fund-raising events.

The effectiveness of promotional products is clear. Research shows that customers, both new and old, who receive promotional products return sooner and reorder more quickly and more frequently than those who receive no promotional incentives.

Benefits of Promotional Product Marketing

The key value of promotional products is in their unique ability to carry a message to a well-defined audience. Because the products are useful to and appreciated by the recipients, they are retained and used, repeating the imprinted message many times without added cost to the advertiser.

Promotional products have the following attributes. They:

- *Are flexible:* You can offer a wide variety of items to various target markets. They can be useful, commemorative, funny, and even controversial.

- *Are tangible and long lasting:* By offering useful and consumable items, recipients are likely to hang onto your gift, many for up to one year.

- *Offer easily measured impact:* You'll know exactly who received your items and, through simple management of your promotional program, you know exactly which items are most effective for your markets.

- *Provide higher perceived value:* Consumers consistently cite the perceived value of promotional products as a key influencer in purchasing decisions, far outweighing the effectiveness of coupons.

- *Complement targeted marketing:* By thoroughly understanding your prospective customers, you can offer items that will appeal to each segment of your demographics.

- *Complement other advertising media:* Promotional products allow you to weave together comprehensive marketing campaigns through a variety of media.

Ready to Get Started?

This book has been developed by marketing experts who specialize in the use of promotional products. Throughout the text, you'll discover real-life success stories about how the creative use of promotional items dramatically impacted the bottom lines of companies big and small. We'll explore step-by-step ways to develop your marketing plan and a comprehensive advertising campaign for any budget. We'll share our expertise on trade shows and maximizing your participation no matter what your goals. Our comprehensive study of sales promotion will help you develop your personalized program for a variety of objectives. We'll also explore the area of public relations and how promotional products can enhance your image in your community. Want to increase enthusiasm and commitment in your own workforce? Our chapter on human resources offers a variety of tips for motivating and rewarding employees. We'll also share our personal collection of trusted resources to eliminate all the guesswork in putting your plan into action right away.

ACKNOWLEDGMENTS

My many clients must be recognized because their case studies are the basis of this book. Thanks are due to the entire team at John Wiley & Sons: Matt Holt, who believed this book would stand out in the crowd and the rest of the Wiley team including Jessica Campilango and Kim Dayman who walked this first-time author through the process.

To authors Joel Bauer and Dave Lakhani who made the necessary introductions to make this project possible.

To my friend Matt Furey who wrote an amazing Foreword for this book.

Last, to all my generous friends who supported me through this year: Robert Adler, Joel and Cherie Bauer, Edna Bowen, David and Simone Brien, Steven Clausen, Don Danielson, Mark and Chris David, Sterling Davis, Darryl Eisner, Mal Emery, Carla Henry, Martin Howey, Annie Kim, Hugh Lipton, Charles Martin, Randal Matz, Hana Na, Vince and Susan Nigro, Orunmila Olodumare, Amparo Polanco, Tabatha Rivera, Chet Rowland, Victor Salerno, Manuel Santana, Lynn Sarkany, Robert and Peggy Schubert, Charles Sevilla, Virpal Sidhu, Janet Switzer, Scott Tucker, Vern Vilmenay, Bob Wall, and Mace Yampolsky.

The Potency of Promotional Products

E. Jerome McCarthy wrote the classic book *Basic Marketing*[1] that defined the four Ps of marketing: product, place, price, and promotion. In order for an organization's marketing strategy to be effective, it must present a high-quality, desirable *product*; the marketing must be delivered to the right *place* to reach targeted clientele who desire the product; the *price* must be in line with the value of the product with consideration given to competitor pricing; but the *power is in the promotion.*

So what is promotion? Product promotion can take the form of advertising, public relations (PR; nonpaid print and broadcast media coverage), grass-roots marketing, and so much more. This book focuses on the astounding effectiveness of spreading the word about a company, service, or product through the innovative use of promotional products.

Promotional products are imprinted or decorated items that are used by businesses and organizations to promote products, services, or company programs. Effective use of promotional products can enhance name and brand recognition, multiply sales, intensify client loyalty, and motivate employees. Furthermore, promotional products are powerful resources that turn an average marketing campaign into a blockbuster promotion. Internally, human resource programs that use promotional products for sales incentives, employee appreciation, and employee gifts

---

[1] William D. Perreault, E. Jerome McCarthy, and colleagues, *Basic Marketing* (Homewood, IL: Richard D. Irwin; 2006).

and awards increase employee loyalty, improve performance, and elevate employee motivation to new heights.

Industry research leader Promotional Products Association International (PPAI) surveyed 839 businesspeople in 1998 about the power of promotional products. An astounding 95 percent of the respondents indicated that they use promotional products in promoting their businesses.[2] And in 2005, PPAI reported that U.S. businesses spent more than $18 billion on promotional products. Some of the most common uses of promotional products include:

- Business gifts
- Dealer/distributor programs
- Trade shows
- Brand awareness improvement campaigns
- Public relations
- New product and service introductions
- New customer recognition
- Account generation
- Not-for-profit programs
- Customer referral programs
- Marketing research incentives
- Internal promotions
- Employee relations and events
- Employee service awards
- Safety and education incentives

Another study conducted by the University of Southern Mississippi for PPAI provided the following list of the top 10 best-selling individual promotional products:

1. Pens
2. Mugs and cups
3. Golf and polo shirts

---

[2] Promotional Products Association International, "The Power of Promotional Products" (1994–2003), www.ppa.org/ProductsResources/Research/_documents/trial.PPT (accessed July 6, 2003).

4. T-shirts
5. Caps and hats
6. Calendars
7. Jackets
8. Key tags and rings
9. Tote bags
10. Mouse pads[3]

The bottom line? If 95 percent of businesses use promotional products to promote their offerings and motivate their employees, chances are your competition is using this effective promotional medium. Therefore, you should be using it, too. But with so many choices of products, suppliers, and programs, where do you begin? Who can you trust?

It's not difficult to begin a promotional products advertising campaign. Using the ideas, tips, and techniques provided in this book, coupled with the expertise of a company that specializes in the design and implementation of customized, high-impact promotional programs (see our suppliers list at the end of the book for recommendations), you can launch a successful promotional program that will skyrocket your profits and performance.

Your Customers Need You

The first and most important step you'll take when embarking on a promotional program is realizing and accepting that your prospects need you. Never feel that you are intruding on prospects. Try to imagine a world without advertising. How would you know where to go to buy parts for your car or furniture for your newly built home? If you are heading out on the town Saturday night, how would you know what's going on, what's happening, and where to go?

Advertising brings information and ideas to the public and, whether they consciously realize it, they appreciate it. Always approach potential customers with the attitude that you are doing them a favor. You are

---

[3] Promotional Products Association International, "The Power of Promotional Products" (1994–2003), www.ppa.org/ProductsResources/Research/_documents/trial.PPT (accessed July 6, 2003).

presenting your products and services to them so they don't have to beat the bushes to find what they need and desire. By using promotional products to reinforce this concept, you give prospective clients a usable item that they will most likely keep, reminding them, maybe even daily, that you have the products and services they want. Consumers won't keep a printed advertisement or even a promotional letter, but a customized calendar puts your contact information at their fingertips every day for an entire year. Need more examples? Imprinted key rings keep your company name fresh on their minds. You're the savior when they are frantically searching for a pen to take down an important message and they reach for one that portrays your company information.

The value of advertising is often expressed in a price per impression. For example, if you place an advertisement in a newspaper, the number of times that newspaper is viewed is the number of impressions you are paying for. However, while newspaper ads reach a vast number of people, they don't repeatedly make an impression on individual prospects in the way that promotional products do. Talk about an excellent price per impression (PPI)—promotional products are *very effective*.

Price per impression starts at just pennies per piece.

Another factor to consider when determining PPI is the frequency of exposure, which can dramatically lower the PPI. According to PPAI, 73 percent of those who used the promotional product that they had received stated that they used it at least once a week, with nearly half of them using it at least once a day. The greater the frequency of exposure, the lower the PPI, thus repeated exposure is important. According to a study conducted by PPAI, 55 percent of participants generally kept their promotional products for more than a year and 22 percent of participants kept the promotional product for at least six months.

The bottom line? Take the time to select promotional products that are useful, memorable, and have lasting quality.

Psychology of Promotion

Walter Dill Scott was an influential figure in the movement to apply scientific psychology to the study of business. One of his primary focuses was on the psychology of advertising. Scott's philosophy was that "advertising has as its one function, influencing the human mind." Scott believed that every normal person is subject to the influence of suggestion and that suggestion, not reason, is the primary determinant of human action. Scott listed four principles that create a memorable advertisement:

1. Repetition
2. Intensity
3. Association value
4. Ingenuity[4]

A study conducted by Southern Methodist University for PPAI showed that, on average, customers who receive promotional products return sooner and more frequently to businesses. In addition, they spend more than customers who receive coupons as a form of promotion.[5] That is solid proof of the power promotional products have on sales and repeat business.

Another realization in the process of promotion is that prospects act on impulse. Because prospects have a busy work life, repetition, intensity, association value, and ingenuity are critical to impulsive buying. For example, imagine that you run a direct-mail campaign to reach your prospects and include a promotional item along with your sales letter. Perhaps a busy executive will open the mailing in the few minutes he has to spare before an important client presentation. He glances at the information in the letter and thinks, "Hmmm, that looks like a great product," but is in a hurry and has no time for impulse buying. So rather than further clutter his desk, he tosses the letter in the trash, but takes the imprinted ink pen that was enclosed along to the meeting. In his hand, your prospect holds your company's contact information. Later, if he recalls your product that seemed interesting, your prospect may call you for information. However, there is a pretty good chance that your prospect won't think about your mailer or company again. It's also possible that your prospect never read the promotional piece to begin with. This underscores the importance of sequential mailings.

---

[4] Robert Wozniak, *Classics in Psychology: Walter Dill Scott—The Psychology of Advertising, 1908,* (1999), www.thoemmes.com/psych/scott.htm (accessed June 24, 2003).

[5] Promotional Products Association International, "Keep Customers Coming Back with Promotional Products" (1994 to 2003), www.ppa.org/ProductsResources/Research/SalesPowerTools/SPT_RepeatBusiness.asp (accessed July 6, 2003).

Sequential Mailings

Sequential mailings give a "remember me?" type of message. The first mailing gets your name, in the form of a promotional product, into the hands of a prospective customer. Sequential mailings reinforce your message. When your prospects open the second mailing, they will have a sense of recognition and are more likely to read the accompanying promotional piece. Perhaps the second mailing included a paperclip dispenser personalized with your company name and logo. This item will sit on their desks, next to your promotional pen, again with your name and contact information. With repetitive mailings, you will have your prospects surrounded by your company name, logo, slogan, and contact information. All of this is key to developing name and brand recognition.

> Surround your potential clients with your promotional products through sequential mailings to increase your name and brand recognition.

Brand Recognition

When you go grocery shopping are you going to buy Planters® Cocktail Peanuts or Uncle Jim's Favorite Peanuts? Well, unless Uncle Jim's peanuts are significantly less expensive and you are a price shopper, you will buy the Planters brand peanuts. The reason for this is name and brand recognition.

For years, Mr. Peanut® has been telling you that Planters Peanuts are the *Best*. And whether you have ever eaten any, you believe him. But if Uncle Jim sends you promotional products repetitively along with promotional letters or fliers promoting his peanuts, you will have items with his name, logo, or slogan in your home or office. Because of the name and brand recognition developed by the promotional products, you may just decide to give Uncle Jim's Peanuts a try, even if you love Planters Peanuts. As a result of brand recognition, reinforced through repetitive delivery of promotional products, you are introduced to a new product. From that point, the quality and value of the actual product becomes important. Another great promotional idea is to send an imprinted "keepable" container filled with a sample of the peanuts. Once the nuts are gone, your prospect will likely continue to use the keepsake container for other uses.

Provide keepsake samples to introduce your product.

Three-time world heavyweight boxing champion Muhammad Ali once said, "I figured that if I said it enough, I would convince the world that I really was the greatest." Perhaps "saying it enough" is the key.

Sales Promotion

In marketing, sales promotion is one of the four aspects of promotion. (The other three parts of the promotional mix are advertising, personal selling, and public relations.) Sales promotions are nonpersonal promotional efforts that are designed to have an immediate impact on sales. Sales promotions use media and nonmedia marketing methods for a predetermined, limited time to increase consumer demand, stimulate market demand or improve product availability. Examples include:

- Coupons
- Discounts and sales
- Contests
- Point of purchase displays
- Rebates

- Free samples
- Gifts and incentive items
- Free travel, such as free flights

Sales promotions can be directed at customers, sales staff, or distribution channel members such as retailers. Sales promotions targeted at the consumer are called *consumer sales promotions*. Sales promotions targeted at retailers and wholesalers are called *trade sales promotions*.

Some purposes of sales promotion include:

- Increasing the distribution of a product or service
- Disposing of inventory to make room for new products
- Expanding the customer base through initial purchases while building repeat customers
- Introducing a new product, service, image, or improvement and new uses for a product or service
- Increasing competitive advantages
- Moving into new target markets
- Adding power to an advertising campaign
- Increasing awareness of a company, product, or service, and name and brand recognition
- Creating desire for a product or service
- Increasing trade channels and goodwill toward the company

Imprinted promotional products can serve as an ice-breaker for new salespeople to meet and greet existing clients or for the salesforce to make cold calls on prospective customers. Promotional products can be used as *premiums* and *freemiums* to encourage purchases or to increase the dollar amount of purchases. Unique "don't forget me" leave-behind imprinted promotional products reinforce sales-promotion efforts. Personalized promotional products can also be used as sales incentives to encourage salespeople to meet sales projections and increase sales. They can be used as thank-you gifts for customers, employees, vendors, and strategic alliances. Sales promotions can be enhanced through the distribution of promotional products in a "customer appreciation" effort that has the potential of increasing customer loyalty.

Trade shows provide an opportunity for businesses and other organizations to meet the public, introduce their products and services, and generate leads. Trade shows are filled with attendees who benefit from the particular product or service you are offering, so the audience is made up of exceptionally targeted clientele. You can always attract trade-show participants to your booth by providing free food or candy; however, those are consumable items that don't stay with them and leave a lasting impression. Distributing promotional products and holding a drawing for high-demand promotional products, such as clothing items or sports bags, flood your trade show booth with traffic and provide visitors with a tangible item that will continue to promote your company after the show has ended.

Shower your trade-show visitors with promotional products to remember you by.

Public Relations

The Public Relations Society of America emphasizes that the publicity and promotional aspect of public relations "paves the way for the sale of products or services."[6] Basically, public relations efforts involve providing internal motivation, building a team spirit inside an organization, and fostering positive interaction between organization or company representatives and the public. Organizations can achieve balance through a public relations program that rewards employees for positive behavior and performance, supports the local community, and promotes solutions to issues of public concern. Positive public relations can be achieved through a variety of venues. Supporting nonprofit, political, and school organizations enhances a company or organization's reputation in the public eye. Sponsoring events such as school registrations, public health seminars, voter registration booths, and similar functions can be accomplished through providing useful products that are needed to conduct the event such as badge holders, pencils, note

---

[6] Public Relations Society of America, "About Public Relations" (2003), www.prsa.org/_Resources/Profession/index.asp?ident=prof1 (accessed July 6, 2003).

pads, folders, or binders; all imprinted with your company information, of course.

We'll explore the particulars of developing a public relations program later in this book.

Enhance your public relations program by providing needed items to support charitable or community events.

Human Resources

Your internal customers, or employees, are just as important, if not more so, than your current and prospective customers. You can develop a unique and effective promotional campaign to drive new customers to your door, but if your employees aren't informed, enthusiastic, and motivated, your money is ill-spent.

In the human resource arena, the use of promotional products is truly unlimited. Imprinted t-shirts, jackets, aprons, tool belts, and such can be used as part of a company uniform that identifies your employees to customers and guests.

Promotional products make outstanding awards, gifts, and incentives to:

- Build morale
- Enhance employee performance and awareness
- Provide much needed recognition
- Foster a team environment
- Increase motivation
- Encourage participation in contests
- Improve safety programs
- Add value to training programs
- Reward outstanding performance or attendance
- Encourage participation in company health programs
- Boost sales

> Use promotional products to add value to your human
> resources program.

Promotional products are effective tools for heightening awareness in all areas of your organization. In this book, we introduce original
ideas and creative campaigns that will prepare you to unleash the *power*
and experience the *potency* of promotional products.

Your Marketing Plan

Many business owners are under the incorrect assumption that by simply placing an ad in a local newspaper or a commercial on a radio or a television station, customers will automatically flock to purchase their product or service. This may be true to a certain extent. Some people are likely to learn about your product or service and try it, just out of curiosity. But hundreds, even thousands, of other potential customers may never learn of your product or business. Therefore, a comprehensive marketing plan is essential to ensure consistency, effectiveness, and cost control. Remember that your goal is not only to attract and keep a steady group of loyal customers, but also to expand your customer base by identifying and attracting new customers and to reduce risks by anticipating market shifts that can affect your bottom line.

Prior to launching an advertising or promotional campaign, an organization should have a solid marketing plan. Marketing plan components are not written in stone and should be open to adjustment, based on your company's changing goals, markets, and budget. However, the following information should generally be included in any marketing plan:

- Analysis of the organization's current situation
- Strengths, weaknesses, opportunities, and threats (SWOT) analysis
- Overview of the competition
- Measurable objectives

- Marketing strategy
- Action programs
- Budget

Current Situation

A comprehensive view of the company's situation includes market research concerning trends, patterns, and critical factors within the industry. Also critical is a thorough overview of the target market, its characteristics, needs, desires, and buying patterns. A complete examination of the competitive environment including identification of competitive advantages and weaknesses, or the SWOT analysis that examines an organization's strengths, weaknesses, opportunities and threats.

Identify and describe your target market by:

- Age
- Sex
- Profession or career
- Income level
- Educational level
- Residence

Know your customers better than you know anyone—their likes, dislikes, hobbies, habits, and expectations. Because you will have limited resources, target only those customers who are most likely to purchase your product. As your business grows and your customer base expands, you may need to consider modifying this section of the marketing plan to include other customers.

Where can you find the information you need to develop your plan? The best sources for industry information are dictated by your particular industry; however, a number of market research firms provide reports including current conditions and historical perspectives in any given industry. For a price, these firms will conduct a customized industry analysis. Although legitimate market-research firms can be very helpful in obtaining the industry information you need for your industry, there may be more efficient and less expensive avenues you can pursue to obtain the information.

Trade organizations and unions often conduct market research on related industries and compile the data for the perusal of industry insiders. Sometimes these reports are free or are provided for minimal fees. Often, trade members can obtain full access to all available materials. This type of membership can be priceless in terms of networking possibilities and industry-specific resources. Industry magazines also provide some statistical information specific to a given industry. Organizations such as the Chamber of Commerce, Department of Development, or Small Business Service Centers can usually provide information about specific industries and target markets.

For businesses operating in the United States, the U.S. Census Bureau is a valuable resource for target-market data. Census data can help determine the size of your target market and their composition in terms of gender, age, ethnicity, marital status, and other demographic data. Census data provides information on the population, its diversity, median incomes, housing status, and spending trends. The U.S. Census Bureau publishes statistics and projections in regard to population growth, income, poverty, housing, and economics in addition to economic statistics and information regarding foreign trade. Census Bureau data is easily obtained through the Internet by visiting the bureau's web site (see the Resource Guide at the end of the book for more information).

If your company is global or Internet based, industry information and target-market statistics may be a little harder to obtain. However, the U.S. Census Bureau does publish information and statistics regarding foreign trade. The Internet is also an astounding source for statistics and industry and competitor information.

An excellent method for obtaining information on the target market's requirements is to ask them. This can be accomplished through a study using focus groups, one-on-one consumer interviews, a poll, or a survey. Obtaining comments, suggestions, and feedback from your target audience can boost your marketing program in terms of product, price, and place, as well as assisting you in determining the best forms of promotion for your company. Focus groups are a powerful means to evaluate services or test new ideas. Many organizations specialize in focus-group research. This service may be valuable if you are introducing a product or service nationwide or have other broad-reaching programs. You can also create your own focus group using current, former, and prospective customers. Participants are generally rewarded with payment of cash, products, or services.

Focus groups generally consist of people whose characteristics are similar to those of your target market. The optimal size of a focus group is dependent on your objectives; however, 10 to 15 members is common. These groups can provide valuable insight because group meetings and discussions introduce fresh and innovative concepts and allow you to probe for the reasons behind the comments, suggestions, and discussion. They enable you to obtain more information than simple answers to questions.

Surveys can be conducted by mail, e-mail, or telephone and can be targeted toward customers or potential customers. An effective survey asks simple questions that are very specific. Surveys can certainly be conducted by in-house staff, but it may be more cost effective and productive to outsource the process to a firm that specializes in conducting surveys and analyzing the generated data. The disadvantage of surveys is lack of participation. A low-response rate will not provide data that is representative of the target market; therefore, tactics must be employed to encourage participation. A reward in the form of a premium can certainly encourage participation in a survey, increasing the effectiveness and usability of the data obtained. It is important to accurately identify the audience for the survey and write the survey in a manner that elicits required information without creating confusion. If a survey contains identifiable information, the results can also be used for lead generation.

Identify Your Competition

Identify the five nearest direct and indirect competitors. Research the weaknesses and strengths of each. Keep files on their advertising and promotional materials and pricing strategies. Review these files periodically to determine when and how often they advertise, sponsor promotions, and offer sales.

Identify your competition by:

- Market research data
- Demand for product
- Your nearest direct and indirect competitors
- Strengths and weaknesses of competitors
- Assessment of how competitors' businesses are doing
- Description of the unique features of your product
- Similarities and dissimilarities between your product and the competitor's
- Comparing your pricing strategy to the competition's

A competitive analysis involves identifying your primary competitors and fully analyzing their operations including their product and/or services; price and value; delivery; guarantees and policies. SWOT (strengths, weaknesses, opportunities and threats) analyses, conducted in regard to your competitors can be compared to your internal SWOT analysis to assist with the identification or development of competitive advantages. In developing your advertising and promotional programs, these competitive advantages and an explanation of how they meet identified needs of the target market better than the competition will be the foundation of your campaigns.

Describe Your Product

Try to describe the benefits of your product(s) from your customers' perspective. Emphasize its special features or selling points. Successful business owners know or at least have an idea of what their customers want or expect from them. This type of anticipation can be helpful in building customer satisfaction and loyalty.

Describe Location (Place)

Again, try to describe the location of your business from your customers' perspective. Describe its assets such as convenience, whether public transportation is accessible, the safety aspects including street lighting, well-lit parking lot or facility, decor, and so on. Your location should be built around your customers. It should be accessible and should provide a sense of security. Be sure to include:

- Description of the location
- Advantages and disadvantages of location

Pricing Strategy

Although your pricing strategy may be based on the strategy devised by others, you should study this plan and the strategies used by competitors. That way you will acquire a thorough understanding of how to price your product, and you can determine if your prices are in line with competitors, if they are in line with industry averages, and what adjustments you can make to bring them into line.

The key to success is to have a well-planned strategy, to establish your policies, and to constantly monitor prices and operating costs to ensure profits. Keep abreast of changes in the marketplace because these changes can affect your bottom line. Areas to consider include:

- Pricing techniques and a brief description of these techniques
- Retail costing and pricing
- Competitive position
- Pricing below competition
- Pricing above competition
- Material costs
- Labor costs
- Overhead costs

Measurable Objectives

Benjamin Franklin once said, "Living without a goal is like shooting without a target." Marketing objectives are individual components that lead to the realization of company goals. The development of measurable objectives as part of your marketing plan will guide your marketing efforts and provide benchmarks by which you can track your progress and measure the success of your marketing programs. Objectives should be very specific. For example, if your company goal is to increase sales by 20 percent over a six-month period, your marketing objectives should be aligned with that goal. Your marketing objectives may include short-term goals such as increasing sales by 5 percent per month over a six-month period in addition to long-term goals to maintain or further escalate sales volume. To reach organizational goals, you may have more individualized marketing objectives such as penetrating a new market, increasing the customer base, or developing strategic partnerships. Whatever the objectives are, they must be measurable with stated milestones in order to track your progress and determine the effectiveness of your programs. Larger organizations often find that goals by department and even employee help further drive success for the company as a whole.

Goals and objectives keep an organization focused on an end result; furthermore, measurements facilitate recognition of shortfalls, enabling an organization to take corrective actions to ensure fulfillment of its overall purpose.

Marketing Strategy

In the most basic terms, marketing strategy is the means for reaching the goals and objectives set forth in the business and marketing plans. The overall goal is generally related to income, increasing sales. This can be accomplished by growth of the customer base, establishment of repeat customers with frequent repurchases or an increase in per-transaction expenditure. In a nonprofit agency, the goals may not be financially based and may focus more on generating volunteer manpower to accomplish nonfinancial objectives. This section of the plan contains short- and long-term strategies to gain customers, increase sales volume, and retain those customers to provide repurchases.

Attracting New Customers

Growth of the customer base can be accomplished by attracting new customers, obtaining referrals from existing customers, and establishing repeat customers. One method for attracting new customers is to offer products as an incentive. For example, an office-supply company may send a catalog to prospects featuring a first-time customer incentive on the cover. Because the prospects are probably businesspeople, a portfolio or a briefcase would be an ideal promotional offering. A purchaser of office supplies will realize that pricing among suppliers is comparable, but if they order from you, they will receive a useful item of value in addition to the office supplies that they would purchase anyway. The promotional product will encourage them to order from you, even if your prices are slightly higher than the competition. Furthermore, once you get the first order and service it efficiently, the new customer is more likely to return to your company again.

> Use first-time buyer incentives to grow your customer base.

Retaining Current Customers

Experts agree that it is easier (and less expensive) to retain a customer than to attract a new one. Customers who have a good experience with your company will not only come back, they will provide referrals. With that in mind, your marketing strategy should incorporate customer appreciation programs. Promotional products such as logo-imprinted business card holders, clipboards, or coffee mugs can be included with reorders along with a personal note thanking your customers for their order and loyalty. They will appreciate the personal touch and the product. Plus, it leaves a lasting impression.

Retain your customers through a customer appreciation program.

Customer Referral Programs

Word-of-mouth advertising is one of the most productive methods to develop a customer base. Customer referral programs, using promotional product incentives, encourage your current customers to refer family, friends, and associates. To implement a customer referral program, you inform your customers that they will receive a desirable promotional product such as a stereo, tool kit, or set of steak knives for each customer they refer who places an order.

While customer appreciation and customer referral programs are important for expanding your customer base, take care not to forget your existing customers who are your bread and butter. Incorporating repeat purchase incentives into your marketing strategy is an excellent way to keep your valued customers coming back with frequent repurchases.

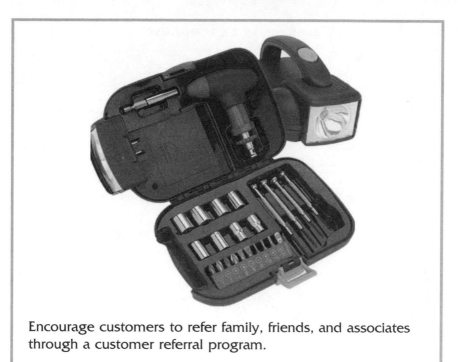

Encourage customers to refer family, friends, and associates through a customer referral program.

Capture repeat purchases to boost sales.

Increasing Per-Transaction Expenditure

Even small increases in transaction amounts can substantially increase your revenue. Suppose that you make 20 sales in one day and each sale averages $75. With a per-transaction increase of $25, you will generate an additional $500 in revenue in one day. That adds up to about $15,000 a month or more than $185,000 a year!

But how can you entice customers to spend more with every transaction? Here's where promotional product incentives can sky-rocket your sales. If a customer is already spending $75, and you offer an incentive gift for a $100 purchase, she is likely to add another case of paper, extra print cartridge, or other item to her order to qualify for the free gift. She ends up with everything she needs, plus a gift for herself or someone else.

> Multiply your revenue using novelties and gifts to increase transaction amounts.

Action Plan and Budget

Action plans designate the time line and individual marketing efforts that will implement your marketing strategy and fulfill your marketing objectives. The marketing budget is the determination of how much money you will spend on marketing and how it will be spent.

Action Plan

You've researched your target markets, explored the strengths and weaknesses of your competitors, outlined your product offerings and pricing, and established measurable goals. Now you need to put everything in writing, establishing a master document that will keep every member of your company on the same page, adhering to a comprehensive plan that identifies your message, marketing mediums, time lines, and budget. Now, the secret to creating an effective marketing plan is to break it down into manageable chunks by creating mini-marketing plans. Each brief, action-oriented mini-plan addresses the various areas of your marketing plan. Your action plan should include the following mini-plans:

- *Publicity:* Identify the activities and promotions that you'll do to spread the word about you and your business through the media. This includes pitching stories to the press, writing press releases on a consistent basis, supporting local charitable events and organizations, and more. We'll explore this in detail in a later chapter.

- *Promotional Events:* Include various promotional activities such as contests, awards, customer appreciation events, trade shows, and more.

- *Joint Venture Marketing:* If you can work with other businesses to promote your business, outline your programs here. For example, if you are a restaurant owner, you could team up with a local movie or live theatre to offer special pretheatre dining promotions or movie-related giveaways.

- *Referral Marketing:* We've discussed the importance of customer referrals for generating new business. Your referral marketing plan should include specifics about the referral programs that you plan to roll out throughout the year.

- *Internet Marketing:* A Web presence is essential for even small companies. Customers often rely on the existence of a web site (no matter how simple) to validate the credibility of a company. You can set up your own web site using user-friendly services available through a variety of sources or look for an experienced designer to assist you in your web site creation and promotion.

- *Advertising:* Not every business advertises but most do, so you should plan where you're going to advertise and how much advertising you'll be doing.

- *Customer Marketing:* How are you going to keep in touch with your current customers? What types of special promotions will you target to them throughout the year?

These aren't the only components of your action plan that you should be thinking about. Service providers will probably have a networking plan, public speaking program, volunteer charity, or association involvement plan. The key is to break down your overall marketing plan into bite-sized mini-plans that help you crystallize what it is you're trying to accomplish.

Now you'll need to put your mini-plans into a month-by-month, week-by-week, or even day-by-day schedule. This plan will include an itemized list of all programs, mediums, and staffing that you will use to reach your target markets. Clearly defining these essential programs, the time line for implementing them, and the resources required in addition to including them in your marketing budget ensures that your marketing program remains focused and generates the response required to reach your goals.

Budget

Marketing budgets vary widely from business to business, ranging from less than 1 percent of net sales for industrial business-to-business operations to 10 percent or more for companies marketing consumer-packaged goods. In fact, some consumer companies may spend 50 percent of net sales for introductory marketing programs in the first year, subsequently lowering the percentage spent to a stable 8 to 10 percent within a few years. Retail stores that advertise and promote spend an average of 4 to 6 percent of net sales for marketing support.

Often, small businesses estimate their sales revenue, cost of goods, overhead, and salaries, and then gross profit. Anything left is considered available funds for marketing. That's not such a good idea. A more rational approach for setting your marketing budget is to estimate what your direct competitors spend in marketing support and then try to at least match that amount. And if you are the new competitor in the marketplace, you will have to spend more to aggressively establish your market share objective.

The most important thing to remember when establishing your budget is that marketing success is a direct result of creativity, not necessarily a big budget.

Advertising

So, what is advertising anyway? Biographer, novelist, and theater critic John Lahr has an interesting viewpoint in regard to advertising, saying that "society drives people crazy with lust and calls it advertising."

Jef I. Richards, Chairman of the University of Texas Advertising Department and accomplished author enlightens us with the following definition: "Creative without strategy is called 'art.' Creative with strategy is called 'advertising.'"

Merriam-Webster offers the following definitions:

- "To make something known to: notify"
- "To make publicly and generally known"
- "To announce publicly especially by a printed notice or a broadcast"
- "To call public attention to especially by emphasizing desirable qualities so as to arouse a desire to buy or patronize: promote"[1]

While advertising is a complex concept, it is essentially a means of informing the public about products and services in an attempt to create desire and ultimately promoting companies, products, and services to produce sales. There are a number of mediums for advertising including television, radio, newspapers, magazines, direct mail, e-mail, e-zines—the list goes on and on. Effective advertising consists of a balance of

---

[1] *Merriam-Webster Online*, s.v. "advertising," www.m-w.com/cgi-bin/dictionary?book=Dictionary&va=advertising (accessed July 6, 2003).

advertising mediums. This balance varies by target market, goals, offerings, and available budget.

Promotional products complement and enhance any advertising campaign by providing a tangible, useful, and desirable item to customers and prospects that is imprinted with your company information and logo. The item is invaluable to you because it reminds them of your company day after day.

Advertising Basics

Regardless of the size of your business, an understanding of the laws of advertising can reap huge rewards. And whether you develop your program yourself or use an outside consultant, the principles remain the same:

- *Use One Message:* A high response rate ad usually conveys a single message. Your advertising needs to quickly communicate its core message in three seconds or less.

- *Ad Credibility:* It has become human nature to distrust advertising. Claims need to be real and credible. Roy H. Williams, best-selling author of the *Wizard of Ads* says, "Any claim made in your advertising which your customer does not perceive as the truth is a horrible waste of ad dollars." Testimonials from customers add enormous credibility to your promotion.

- *Test Everything:* Large businesses have a greater margin to waste capital and resources without testing advertising. Small businesses do not have that luxury. Testing can be as simple as asking every customer for several weeks how they heard of your business.

- *Be Easy to Contact:* Every single brochure, box, e-mail, and all company literature (letterhead, invoices, business cards, etc.) should have full contact information including Web and e-mail addresses, phone and fax numbers, and company address. It seems simple but is forgotten by most companies. If you have a tag line, be sure it is also included on every piece of communication.

- *Match Ads to Target:* Successful business advertising speaks to one target market only. Focus the message to the target group's needs, wants, desires, fears, and so on.

- *Create Curiosity:* Successful business advertising does not sell a product or service. Create ads that generate interest, driving the customer to contact you for more information.

Sequential Mailings

In the Preface, we touched on the power of sequential mailings and surrounding your prospects with imprinted promotional products to keep your name in the forefront of their minds and lives. Here we provide some practical examples of sequential mail letters that can be used to accomplish this mission. For the purpose of demonstration, we will use a hypothetical insurance company; however, these sample letters can be easily adapted to work for any industry. You print the letter on your company letterhead.

Direct Mail Example One: Introduction Letter

Dear Friend,

XYZ Insurance would like to invite you to receive a free insurance review. Many consumers make the fatal mistake of purchasing automatically renewing insurance policies and paying the premiums consistently month after month, never taking the time to reevaluate their insurance coverage in relation to changes in circumstances. When those unwelcome catastrophes hit, they are unprepared because their policies are not sufficient to meet their current needs.

To ensure that this doesn't happen to you, please contact our professional insurance assessment team at 555-555-5555 and request a complimentary insurance review to make sure that you have adequate coverage to withstand any unexpected occurrence.

Thank you in advance for your time and for placing your trust in XYZ Insurance to ensure a stable future for you and your family.

Sincerely,

John Doe, Insurance Agent

Enclose an imprinted ink pen with the first contact letter to ensure that your prospect will open it.

Direct Mail Example Two: First-Time Buyer Discounts

Dear Friend,

XYZ Insurance realizes the importance of comprehensive insurance coverage for your family including homeowner's, vehicle, life, health and disability insurance. To assist you in ensuring that your family has adequate protection in all areas of your life, we are offering a **first-time buyer's discount** of **10 percent off your annual premium**.

By taking advantage of this offer, you can obtain all the necessary coverage for your family to ensure that you are adequately covered in case of a disaster or health crisis. The discount offered by XYZ Insurance will enable you to purchase better coverage at a lower rate.

For a full family insurance review and rate quote, please contact our customer service department today at 555-555-5555.

Sincerely,

John Doe, Insurance Agent

Enclose an imprinted keychain with your second contact letter.

Direct Mail Example Three: Industry News

Dear Friend,

Because we care about you and your family, XYZ Insurance would like to share some exciting news! We now have dental insurance plans starting at only $9 per month! The coverage pays up to 70 percent of dental expenses ranging from check-ups to major dental procedures.

Call our customer service department today for more information about this awesome coverage for your family.

Sincerely,

John Doe, Insurance Agent

Send an imprinted family gift with your third contact letter.

Direct Mail Example Four: New Year's Letter

Dear Friend,

Start the New Year off right with an insurance evaluation from XYZ Insurance. Don't go another year with inadequate insurance protection for your family and your assets. The professional analysts at XYZ Insurance can evaluate your entire insurance portfolio and make suggestions to enhance your coverage while minimizing the cost of insurance for you and your family.

A comprehensive analysis of your family insurance coverage is absolutely free and it can give you peace of mind knowing that your home, your vehicles, and your family are adequately covered and you will be able to sustain any crisis or catastrophe that presents itself.

To receive your free insurance analysis, contact our customer service department today at 555-555-5555. Have a happy and prosperous New Year!

Sincerely,

John Doe, Insurance Agent

Enclose an imprinted calendar with your New Year's letter.

Sequential mailing can also be accomplished through an inexpensive e-mail advertising campaign. The process is similar; however, rather than sending imprinted promotional products, you provide a promotional product incentive touted in the description line of the e-mail to encourage recipients to open the message and respond. Some samples of sequential e-mail letters follow.

E-mail Example One: Introduction Letter

Dear Friend,

ABC Office Supply would like to invite you to experience the best service and best prices for a comprehensive line of first-rate office supplies. Visit our web site at www.ABC.com to view our

(Continued)

online catalog and request a print catalog by mail. When requesting your print catalog, enter the reference 114 to receive our convenient travel kit in the mail along with your catalog.

ABC Office Supply

As a first-time buyer, if you choose to place an order with ABC Office Supply today, you will automatically receive a luxurious and functional briefcase as a gift and expression of our appreciation.

Thank you for your time and attention! We look forward to serving all your office supply needs!

Sincerely,

Jane Doe, CEO

E-mail Example Two: Special Offer

Re: A FREE portable television just for you!

Dear Friend,

We are excited to announce a new promotion that you will absolutely love! For a limited time, ABC Office Supply is offering new credit customers a FREE portable television that is a perfect companion for those long, often boring, business trips. To claim your free television, visit our web site at www.ABC.com/credit and complete our secure online corporate credit application. Once your application is submitted, you will be qualified to receive this outstanding gift. Plus, a credit account with ABC Office Supply will simplify and expedite your office supply purchases.

Act now! Supplies are limited!

ABC Office Supply is a leading provider of discount office supplies and products. Our quantity discounts allow you to keep the items you most need on-hand at all times while providing the best prices in the office supply market today! When comparing prices, be sure to take into account that ABC Office Supply offers free shipping on orders over $30. We look forward to serving all your office supply needs AND saving you money!

Sincerely,

Jane Doe, CEO

> ## E-mail Example Three: Holiday Letter
>
> Re: A FREE camera from ABC Office Supply!
>
> Dear Friend,
>
> Certainly you are busy preparing for the holiday season and the last thing you need on your to-do list is shopping for employees and corporate clients. Rest assured that ABC Office Supply has got you covered. We have a full line of office products, furniture, décor, computers, technology accessories and highly demanded electronic items.
>
> An ABC Office Supply Holiday Gift Certificate is certain to suffice your gift giving needs, plus we take care of the details for you! Visit our site at www.ABC.com and order your gift certificates online. We'll wrap and deliver your gifts for you by December 24, helping you remove another item from your busy holiday list of things to do!
>
> Additionally, if you purchase $150 or more in gift certificates, we will send you a FREE 35MM CAMERA that you can keep for yourself or give to someone special as a gift. We look forward to assisting you with all your holiday gift giving needs!
>
> Sincerely,
>
> Jane Doe, CEO

Direct Mail

Direct mail is one of the most powerful methods in existence for marketing your business. This year alone, there will be more than $30 billion spent on direct mail. If it didn't work, there wouldn't be so much money spent on it. The advantage of direct mail is it is completely measurable, targetable, and accountable.

Direct mail consists of marketing communications sent to customers (both current and prospective) through the postal service. Direct mail allows the marketer to design marketing pieces in many different formats ranging from postcards and letters to packages and unique formats including bottles, coconuts, and even miniature trash cans.

If there is this much money and resources devoted to direct mail, why do so many small businesses think of direct mail as a waste or junk mail? Simple. They don't understand how to use it. They've never had any education or training on how to use it effectively. They sent out a flier, a postcard, or a letter and got a poor response without learning that there is a science to making it work. They sent their mailing to a "weak" list. The list you send your mailing to is one of the important tenets to a successful mailing.

The purpose of this section is to demonstrate how promotional products can help you increase the success of your direct-mail program. Experts agree that the use of promotional products increases response rates when used in conjunction with print ad campaigns. In a study conducted by PPAI, some subjects were mailed only a trade ad while others received the same sales letter in addition to a promotional product. Others were sent a promotional product incentive along with the trade ad. The response rate for the trade ad alone was 0.7 percent. The personalized direct-mail letter resulted in a response rate of 2.3 percent, typical of standard direct-mail programs. The response rate increased to 4.2 percent when a promotional product, a stress ball, was included with information similar to letter. With a direct mail package that contained a promotional product incentive for a calculator, the response rate rose to 9.55 percent. Two-thirds of the respondents who received the trade ad and direct mail indicated that the direct-mail piece prompted their response.[2]

So what does this all mean? The inclusion of a promotional product to a mail promotion increased the response rate by 50 percent. Furthermore, the use of promotional products as an incentive to respond generated four times as many responses as a sales letter alone. Therefore, the use of a promotional product as an incentive to respond reduced the cost per response by two-thirds.

These results are absolutely phenomenal. A direct-mail piece with a promotional product increased response rates from 0.7 percent to 4.2 percent and a direct-mail package with a promotional product incentive kicked the response all the way up to 9.55 percent. That is the power of promotional products as a complement to a print advertising campaign.

> Use direct-mail promotional products and promotional product incentives to complement your print advertising campaign and significantly improve response rates.

[2]Promotional Products Association International, "Improve Response Rates to an Advertising Campaign with Promotional Product Mailings" (1994–2003), www.ppa .org/MediaInformation/IndustryStatistics/SalesPowerTools/SPT_AdCampaign.asp (accessed July 7, 2003).

Benefits and Advantages

Direct mail has many advantages. According to the U.S. Census Bureau's March 2000 *Current Population Reports*, there were 12 million single-parent families in the United States. Between 1970 and 2000, single-mother families increased from 3 million to 10 million and single-father families rose from 393,000 to 2 million.[3] According to the report, 31 percent of married-couple households were made up of dual-income families with children and 25 percent of American homes featured dual-income couples without children.[4]

What does all this mean? In our modern lifestyle, people are busy. Most parents work, take care of household responsibilities, and care for children including participation in time-consuming but enjoyable extra-curricular activities. There's homework to help with, church services to attend, shopping to do, voluntary services to support, and the list goes on and on. People are too occupied to take notice of traditional advertising; however, you can bet they all check their mail. And while typical junk mail goes straight to the trash unopened, promotional products can ensure that your piece is opened right away. Studies show that consumers are less likely to toss a mail piece if it appears that something is in it rather than a standard message. We call this dimensional or lumpy mail. After all, enticing a prospect to open the mail piece is half the battle. This is why response rates improve when promotional products are sent along with the direct-mail advertisement.

Another advantage of direct mail is that you can specifically pinpoint your target audience and that you will obtain measurable results to determine program effectiveness, cost-per-order, and cost-per-contact (price per impression). You know how many contacts you made, with whom, how many responses you received, and the cost of every contact. You can determine the amount of repeat business and income provided by a mail campaign or sequential mailings.

---

[3] Jason Fields and Lynne M. Casper, "America's Families and Living Arrangements: March 2000," in *Current Population Reports* (Washington, DC: U.S. Census Bureau, 2001): 20–537.

[4] Ameristat, "Traditional Families Account for Only 7 Percent of U.S. Households" (2003), *Population Reference Bureau*, www.ameristat.org/Content/NavigationMenu/Ameristat/Topics1/MarriageandFamily/Traditional_Families_Account_for_Only_7_Percent_of_U_S__Households.htm (accessed July 11, 2003).

Unlike mass media in which your marketing is conducted in the public eye, direct mail allows you to communicate directly with your customers and prospects, leaving your competition wondering what you are doing. There's nothing more frustrating in the world of business than to launch a unique marketing campaign and have your competitors immediately counter it with something identical or more appealing. Consider traditional holiday sales promotions. When everyone is advertising slashed prices or special offers in the local papers, you can stand out in the crowd by placing your message directly in the hands and homes of your target customer.

Another definite advantage of direct mail is its flexibility. Direct mail containing promotional product incentives can be prepared and sent out quickly. This can help announce a seasonal promotion or even counteract a competitor's promotional efforts. For example, if you are a grocer and your competitor runs an advertisement offering a 20 percent discount on hamburger meat for Independence Day cookouts, you can quickly counter that offer through a direct-mail campaign that offers a free set of barbecue accessories with the purchase of two cases of ready-made hamburger patties or a free grill with the purchase of five or more cases. Your incentive may be more appealing to the general public because it provides convenience with ready-made patties in addition to useful promotional products that they can keep.

Be creative when countering competitors' special offers.

Demographic data allows you to create a highly targeted direct-mail campaign, delivering your advertisements directly to the potential customer's door. This is more personal and compelling than mass media advertising. In a direct-mail campaign, prospects can be targeted by zip code, household income, family size, age, gender, occupation, education level, hobbies, leisure time activities, clubs, organizations, industry classification, size and revenue of businesses, number of employees, or locations.[5] See the Resource Guide at the end of the book for recommended suppliers and information sources.

---

[5]United States Postal Service "Using Direct Mail: Pinpoint Marketing" (2003), www.usps.com/directmail/dmguide/discoverdm/pinpoint.htm (accessed July 17, 2003).

Product Partnerships

Developing cooperative direct-mail marketing partnerships with companies that provide products that complement yours can stretch your marketing budget while instilling a sense of convenience in prospects who receive your mail pieces. For instance, if you sell computers, you may partner with a company that provides peripherals such as printers and another company that publishes software. All three companies can share the expense of a direct-mail campaign, each offering a promotional product incentive for purchases. You can provide a free ergonomic mouse-pad station with a built-in calculator as an incentive to purchase a computer while the printer manufacturer offers a free computer tool kit with the purchase of a printer and the software company provides an incentive for a free computer terms dictionary. The customer who is shopping for a new computer system will see both value and convenience in these three packaged offers.

Team up and use creative, complementary promotional products to make the most of your marketing dollar and portray value to prospects.

E-Mail Marketing

E-mail marketing is one of the most powerful marketing tools available to businesses of all types and sizes. According to the Direct Marketing Association, more than half of small businesses rated e-mail as the number-one online promotion to drive site visitors and customers to their web sites and storefronts.

Why Is E-Mail Marketing so Effective?

It's Inexpensive

E-mail marketing is an affordable way to stretch a tight marketing budget. Unlike direct mail, there is virtually no production, materials, or postage expense. E-mail marketing can cost as little as fractions of a penny per e-mail.

It's Effective

E-mail marketing allows you to proactively communicate with your existing customers and prospects instead of just waiting for them to find or return to your web site or storefront. It is a highly effective way to increase sales, drive site or store traffic, and develop loyalty.

It's Immediate

E-mail marketing generates an immediate response. The call to action is clear: "Click here to take advantage of this offer," or "to learn more about this service." In fact, studies show that initial campaign response generally occurs within 48 hours of the time the e-mail contact is sent.

It's Targeted

You can easily segment your lists using a variety of criteria or interest groups so that your promotions go to the individuals most likely to respond to your offer.

It's Easy

There are many Web-based e-mail marketing products for small and medium businesses. Most include professional HTML templates, list segmentation, and targeting capabilities, as well as, automatic tracking and reporting. Alternatively, you can develop your own e-mail messages, making them as simple or complex as you wish.

The overriding disadvantage of e-mail marketing is that you can't send the promotional product that encourages the receiver to open the mail. Therefore, you have to be extremely creative with your description line. Promotional product incentives can encourage prospects to open the e-mail and read your offer. For example, on the description line, you may print "Receive a *Free*" . . . gift basket with wine, pair of binoculars, New Yorker jacket, leather briefcase, and so on. The possibilities are endless. Another alternative is to offer more expensive promotional products such as televisions through an "opportunity to win" rather than as a free gift.

> Use promotional product incentives to improve e-mail response rates.

Anti-Spam Laws and E-Mail Marketing

No discussion of e-mail marketing would be complete without a discussion of legal aspects, so let's just get it out of the way, shall we? The following recommendations are based on marketing, not legal, experience. You may wish to consult with your attorney or other experts to determine the most current laws and how they related to your marketing. E-mail markcting has its challenges in this world of spam, but there's no need to worry, much less panic, about your e-mail marketing efforts. It is a whole lot easier than you may think to be in compliance with the law.

A lot of recent anti-spam legislation is intended to stop spammers, not to stop legitimate, permission-based e-mailers like you. Right now every state has different laws on the books and pending approval. While federal laws are proposed, no blanket laws exist so each state has its own definition of unsolicited commercial e-mail. Therefore, the best idea is to comply with the strictest standards that are standard among the states. The good news is that all of the existing statutes and pending legislation recognize your right to send e-mail to people with whom you have a preexisting business relationship and those who otherwise consent to receive your e-mail communications.

So what constitutes a preexisting business relationship? These are people who have made a purchase, requested information, responded to a questionnaire or a survey, or had offline contact with you.

And what constitutes consent? These people have been clearly and fully notified of the collection and use of their e-mail addresses and have agreed prior to such collection and use. This is often called *informed consent.*

To make sure you are in compliance with existing laws, follow these simple guidelines:

- Use good permission policy (have a preexisting business relationship and informed consent).
- Evaluate your list and determine the sources of your e-mail addresses.
- Keep a record of the source of each e-mail address you add to your list.
- Use good mailing practices (be honest/truthful).
- Use a subject line that accurately reflects the content of your message.
- Use a legitimate header.
- Use a valid from address.
- Include a working unsubscribe/opt-out link and/or instructions.
- Include your physical address and telephone number.

Advertising

Advertising is often confused with marketing, public relations, or promotions. Most simply, advertising is a paid placement of information that attempts to influence the buying behavior of your customers by providing a persuasive selling message about your products and/or services. There are many different types of advertising including signage, Yellow Pages listings, newspaper advertising, radio and television spots, and Internet advertising through banners, sponsored links, and more.

Before launching any advertising campaign, it's important to understand its advantages and disadvantages.

Advertising can:

- Remind customers and prospects about the benefits of your product or service.
- Establish and maintain your unique identity.
- Enhance your reputation.
- Encourage existing customers to buy more of what you sell.
- Attract new customers.
- Slowly build sales to boost your bottom line.
- Promote your business to customers, investors, and others.

Advertising cannot:

- Create an instant customer base.
- Cause an immediate sharp increase in sales.
- Solve cash-flow or profit problems.
- Substitute for poor or indifferent customer service.
- Sell useless or unwanted products or services.

Advantages and Disadvantages

There are two distinct advantages to advertising. First, you have complete control. Unlike public relations, you determine exactly where, when, and how often your message will appear, how it will look, and what it will say. You can target your audience more readily and aim at very specific geographic areas. Second, you can be consistent, presenting your company's image and sales message repeatedly to build awareness and trust. Customers will recognize you quickly and easily in ads, mailers, packaging, or signs if you present yourself consistently.

Sound good? Advertising also has some distinct disadvantages. First, it requires much planning. Advertising is most effective and costs less when planned and prepared in advance. For example, you'll pay less per ad in newspapers and magazines by committing up-front to a series of ads run over time, rather than placing them one at a time. Likewise, you can save money on graphic design and copywriting by creating a number of ads at once. Second, advertising takes time and persistence. The effectiveness of your advertising improves gradually over time because customers don't see every one of your ads. You must repeatedly remind prospects and customers about the benefits of doing business with you. The long-term effort triggers recognition and helps special offers or direct marketing pay off.

Increasing Effectiveness with Promotional Products

Promotional products can be also be used to increase advertising response rates. Promotional product incentives and drawings for high-dollar promotional products can encourage those exposed to your television, radio, Internet, or newspaper advertisement to respond.

Impulse buying in response to value propositions is human nature. Basic sales tactics are based on the understanding that selling is an emotional evocation. Good salespeople know that most purchases are based on emotion rather than logic. If you have the ability to attract a potential customer's attention and capture his or her interest, you can work on creating desire and prompting action. Promotional product incentives used in conjunction with your advertisements unleash this ability. Free promotional products or an opportunity to win a larger prize attracts attention and sparks interest. The desire for the promotional product prompts action and encourages prospects to become buyers. The bottom line? Offer promotional products that appeal to prospects in order to convert them to customers.

To select the most potent promotional products to complement your media campaign, you need to uncover your prospects' interests. Studying market research such as consumer buying patterns can enlighten you on your target audience's passions. What's hot and what's not? Accurately answering this question can start your promotional product campaign on the road to success. This information varies by target market, geographical region, and more. Talk with your current customers to see what appeals to them. Ask friends and family what they would like to receive. The more real-life research you do, the more effective your promotion will be.

Using desirable promotional products in advertising converts prospects to buyers.

Web Site Marketing

Before the Internet, business owners marketed through expensive advertising and brochures, direct mail, cold-calling, networking at the local Chamber of Commerce, and other grassroots methods.

Owners hoped for word-of-mouth recommendations or a unique ad in the Yellow Pages. Today, the Internet is a source of information, recommendations, and so much more. In the Internet age, prospective customers often find you, rather than you finding them. In this age of the virtual customer, it is highly likely that you'll land a customer that you've never met. It has also made today's consumers especially savvy, with high expectations for a Web presence for even the smallest companies.

According to the International Internet Marketing Association, approximately 68 percent of American adults (128 million people), use the Internet. And more than 75 percent of those ages 12 to 17 are online. The statistics are clear. If you aren't on the Web, you're missing the boat on a major source of prospective clients.

Creating a Credible Impression

The Internet has increased the expectation among consumers that businesses will have a credible online presence. Many consumers form "first impressions" of people and companies via Internet browsers. From the moment your name and business appear in a Web browser to the moment your web site loads, your first impression often means the difference between a shot at your prospect's business, or being shut out. Internet impressions are not just influenced by how your web site looks, but also by how often your business appears or how high it ranks in a Web browser.

Target Markets

The use of web sites is a revolutionary form of marketing to exact targeted clientele. An Internet presence is essential; however, the competition is fast and furious and Internet advertising techniques are evolving very rapidly. The word *free* is one of the most searched keyword terms on the Internet today; therefore, offering "free" products on your web site can drive your search engine rankings up in your market niche. Promotional products are *free*

items that can be used to boost your search engine rankings and attract visitors to your site. In fact, an expert in search optimization reports that the term *free* was searched for 988,138 times during just one month. Among the top phrases searched were "free game," "free clip art," "free music," and "free stuff." Tuning into these top searched keywords can make your web site more visible, increasing your Web traffic and promoting your products and services with free promotional product incentives.

Tune into popular keywords using free promotional products to enhance your Internet presence and the effectiveness of your web site.

4

Trade Show Marketing

A trade show can be a wonderful resource for a small business, bringing new contacts, customers, and ideas.
—Joyce M. Rosenberg[1]

Trade shows are designed to allow businesses to meet many potential customers face-to-face in a brief period of time inexpensively. According to the Trade Show Bureau, more than 4,300 trade shows were held nationwide in 1994, attracting 85 million visitors. Experts agree that trade shows can have a significant impact on a company's bottom line.

A wonderful marketing opportunity for smaller businesses, trade shows can help level the playing field for smaller firms because booth space is generally inexpensive ($13 per square foot on average, with the typical small booth covering 100 square feet), and even small companies can usually afford attractive displays. With creative marketing and booth design, small businesses can actually appear as substantial as much larger corporations.

---

[1] Joyce M. Rosenberg, "Getting the Most of a Trade Show" (2002, October 17), *AP Online*, http://ask.elibrary.com/getdoc.asp?pubname=AP_Online&puburl=http~C~~S ~~S~www.ap.org&querydocid=68788841@urn:bigchalk:U.S.;Lib&dtype=0~0&dinst= 0&author=JOYCE+Mpercent2E+ROSENBERGpercent2C+AP+Business+Writer&title= Getting+the+Most+of+a+Trade+Show++&date=10percent2D17percent2D2002& query=trade+shows&maxdoc=30&idx=26 (accessed July 18, 2003).

According to the Trade Show Bureau, 44 percent of the firms exhibiting at business-to-business shows have fewer than 50 employees. Sophisticated exhibitors do well at trade shows no matter what their size, while the inexperienced can waste thousands of dollars and countless hours and possibly do more harm than good.

There are two basic types of trade shows—business-to-business and consumer. The type of show at which you exhibit is entirely based on the goals of your company. Using trade shows effectively takes only a little effort and planning.

Still not sure if trade shows are ideal for your business? Common reasons for exhibiting include:

- Generating sales leads
- Generating actual sales at the show
- Enhancing your image and visibility
- Targeting a specific audience
- Establishing a presence in the marketplace
- Improving the effectiveness and efficiency of your marketing efforts
- Personally meeting your customers, competitors, and suppliers
- Prospecting for new customers
- Introducing new products and services
- Demonstrating your product in ways not possible using other marketing channels
- Recruiting distributors or dealers
- Educating your target audience.

Maximizing Trade Shows with Promotional Products

A 1991 study indicated that promotional products increase traffic to trade show booths. In the study, an exhibitor sent out 4,900 invitations to registrants. Recipients received between zero and three gifts before, during, and/or after the show. When participants received an invitation to receive a gift at the show, they responded in the form of booth traffic at a higher rate than those that did not receive the offer. The highest response rate came from those who received a gift sent before the show and a matching item at the show. The group that received three promotional products proved to be the most affected by the promotion with 11.6 percent responding, 51 percent remembering the invitation, and 40 percent indicating goodwill toward the company.[2]

Additionally, PPAI reports that 71.6 of attendees who received a promotional product remembered the name of the company that gave them the product. An astounding 76.3 percent of attendees had a favorable attitude toward the company that gave them the product.

Phases of Trade Show Marketing

There are four phases of trade show marketing: planning, preparation, presentation, and follow-up. The first phase, *planning*, encompasses setting goals, selecting a show, organizing the exhibit, and preparing postshow follow-up methods and materials.

Basic *preparation* involves registering for the show, gathering necessary supplies and promotional products, getting promotions and drawings in order, setting up the booth, and staffing it. One key mistake many exhibitors make during the planning phase is neglecting to network with clients and prospects before the show, building antici-pation and incentives to encourage attendance.

The *presentation* is the actual presence at the show and activities that take place during the exhibition. *Follow-up* after the show is essential to realizing the full potential of the show. Trade shows produce excellent leads; however, failing to follow up on those leads, is like forgetting to water seeds you have planted. Next we'll explore the four phases in detail.

Planning

As with any business or marketing venture, it is imperative that you *set clear, measurable goals.* Explicit goals keep you focused and ensure that all your efforts are coordinated, making the most out of your trade show endeavor. What do you want to accomplish at the trade show? Goals might be:

- Attracting a certain number of new retail clients.
- Launching a new or improved product that needs exposure.

---

[2] Promotional Products Association International, "Improve Trade Show Traffic with Promotional Products" (2003), www.ppa.org/ProductsResources/Research/SalesPower Tools/SPT_TradeShows.asp (accessed July 18, 2003).

- Making a certain amount of onsite sales.
- Obtaining a certain number of appointments for one-on-one presentations after the show.

Once you've decided exactly what you want to accomplish through your trade show participation, you can begin planning your strategy.

Selecting the Right Show

Participation in trade shows can be costly, so prior to registering for one, it is essential to research the trade shows that best meet your needs. Trade shows bring targeted traffic to your business; thus it is important that you shoot at the right target. If you are a wholesale supplier of grocery supplies, you want to attend a trade show that attracts retail sellers or users of those grocery products. A trade show with manufacturer exhibitors aimed at wholesaler attendees would be beneficial for you as an attendee, but not as an exhibitor. Find out what the trade show's objectives are and evaluate the show's audience to determine which show best suits your goals and will bring you the best return on your investment. When considering out-of-town shows, be sure to consider additional expenses such as housing, travel, shipping, exhibit rentals, staffing, and so on.

Planning Your Exhibit

After selecting the trade show that will promote your business and fulfill your show goals, book your space. To be prepared, you need to know all there is to know about your space. Where is it located on the show floor? How much room do you have to fill? What types of exhibits are around your space? Is it a high-traffic or low-traffic area? What are the physical attributes of the booth in terms of lighting, electrical outlets, and so on?

If possible, ensure that your booth is in a high-traffic area and that you are not surrounded by competitors. Many show-management companies ask for your preferences regarding the location of your exhibit space so it's important to understand the four basic location categories in any show:

1. *Island:* This location attracts eight lines of sight and is the premier location for any show. It is most often reserved for larger and repeat exhibitors.

2. *End Cap:* This location is exposed to six lines of sight and is also generally saved for larger exhibitors.

3. *Inline:* Exposed to two lines of sight, the best location for inline exhibits is the corner slot.

4. *Perimeter:* These spaces are exposed to two lines of sight and are often assigned to smaller, first-time, or late-registration exhibitors.

Once you know the attributes of your location, you will be prepared to plan the setup of the booth to provide visual appeal to attendees. There are four basic types of displays:

1. *Pipe and Drape:* This display consists of metal pipe which comprises a backwall and side rails. Drapes are attached with velcro. The hall's general contractor usually furnishes this to inline, perimeter, and peninsula booths.

2. *Portable Exhibits:* This type of exhibit is defined by its ease of use. There are two types of portable exhibits—pop-up and tabletop displays. The most commonly used display is the portable pop-up. Available from several manufacturers, this easy-to-set-up display should be ready for use in 15 minutes. It uses a folding aluminum frame and detachable fabric or graphic panels. These units are easily transported, relatively inexpensive, and are designed for the typical 10-foot booth space. A lower-cost version of the pop-up is the tabletop display, which is placed on top of a show-supplied six- to eight-foot draped table. These can be miniature versions of the pop-up display.

3. *Modular Exhibits:* These displays are made of standardized panels with some customization capabilities. Cost is typically higher than pop-ups and they usually require a common carrier for freight in and out of the exhibit hall. Modular systems come in a variety of finishes, from fabric to laminates that can create a very rich look.

4. *Custom Displays:* Generally, these are the most expensive to make and transport. They can be two-storied and command a prominent presence on a show floor.

If you participate in trade shows regularly, you may want to invest in the purchase of an exhibition booth. Customized with your graphics and to your specifications, these booths are attractive and functional.

They simplify and professionalize your display demonstrating to show participants that you are serious about what you do. A rental is a good way to go if you're going to exhibit once a year or if you exhibit internationally. Rentals are usually extremely simple in their design and need to be dressed up with eye-catching graphics. (See our Resource Guide for suppliers.)

> Professional exhibit booths add visual appeal and professionalism to your trade show presence.

When planning your exhibit, view it in through your prospects' eyes. What will attract them to your booth? The answer to that question will guide your efforts. Neatness and visibility should be primary factors in any display. Make sure your company's purpose is immediately clear to anyone looking at your display. Potential clients will walk away from booths if they have to search for the intent of the displayer.

Keep displayed products or literature at eye level and make sure that items for sale are clearly labeled with prices. Attendees expect giveaway items at trade shows. Clearly labeling merchandise that is for sale will keep booth visitors from being embarrassed by accidentally walking away with your for-sale goods.

Create Interest

So how can you make sure that your prospects visit your booth? You must be creative in developing a strategy to make your booth the "exhibit to visit." Interactive displays magnetize your booth, drawing visitors to your exhibit. Contests, games, demonstrations, and similar functions attract attention. Drawings for prizes also entice attendees and are an ideal form of lead generation. The contact information obtained in a drawing can be used for e-mail marketing, direct mail, and follow-up sales calls. Promotional products such as electronics, jewelry, gift baskets, and cookware are excellent items to use in your trade show drawings. Be sure to have the promotional prize on display at the show to generate onsite interest.

> Hold a drawing for promotional products to attract traffic to your trade show booth.

When designing your display, build an image that your products or services are in high demand. This can be done by strategically placing "sold" signs on a few items or leaving a display space empty where it appears that you have been so busy you haven't had time to restock. Consumers are most interested in high-demand items and they'll want to make sure they aren't missing something.

Supplies

Be absolutely certain that you have more than enough sales literature on hand to give to booth visitors. Colored fliers, brochures, price sheets, business cards, and press kits are ideal items to have with you to give to attendees and the trade media. Post important information where it is easily viewed by guests in case you are busy and they have questions. Be sure to have plenty of order forms and sales slips so that you complete sales transactions (if permitted) at the show.

In addition to marketing collateral, have a significant supply of imprinted promotional items to use as giveaways at your booth. All booth staffers should ensure that every visitor walks away with a useful item that will remind them of your company. Of course, pencils, notepads, and coffee mugs are great promotional products; however, you may also want to provide original novelty items. Seeing those "have-to-have" items will send attendees on a quest to find your booth. Place your giveaways so that attendees have to enter your booth to obtain their gift, ensuring they will see your other displays in the process.

Load your trade show guests with imprinted products to keep your company name fresh.

*   *   *

Use novelty and "have-to-have" items to send attendees on a mission to find your booth.

Other ways to attract traffic to your display include offering food, beverages, or candy, either free or for sale. Your booth should be visually attractive. Depending on your image, you may use art, soft music, hard-to-miss signs, bright colors, balloons, inflatables, arrows, or flashing lights to make your booth stand out in the crowd. Playing videos or offering complimentary five-minute neck or foot massages also draw spectators and participants.

Some trade shows offer sponsorship opportunities that place your company's information on imprinted goodie bags or badge holders for every attendee. Others offer gift bags to attendees that feature product samples, brochures, coupons, gifts, and more from select sponsors. Talk with show organizers well in advance of the show to secure your position as an event sponsor.

> Be the center of attention at the trade show by sponsoring the event.

Before the Show

Rob Frankel, a small business consultant in Los Angeles, says that if you fail to start networking before the show, "you've missed out on 80 percent of the value of a trade show."[3] Start promoting your presence at the trade show long before you or your prospects ever hit the exhibit floor. Inform your customers, prospects, suppliers, and other associates that you will be participating in the show and introduce them to the special offers you'll feature. If you have a booth number, be sure to include it in your preshow advertisements so it will be easy for your contacts to find your exhibit. Build anticipation for the event with creative mailings, offers, and opportunities to win large prizes.

The purpose of your preshow marketing and promotion is to get customers and prospects to come to the show and visit your booth. Promotion can be accomplished personally, through direct mail, e-mail, or by media and magazine advertising. Additionally, post fliers, invitations, or brochures at your storefront and hand them out to patrons and insert them in order shipments or packages. Include your participant and promotion information on your web site and in newsletters or

---

[3] Joyce M. Rosenberg, "Getting the Most of a Trade Show" (2002, October 17), *AP Online*, http://ask.elibrary.com/getdoc.asp?pubname=AP_Online&puburl=http~C~~S~~S~ www.ap.org&querydocid=68788841@urn:bigchalk:U.S.;Lib&dtype=0~0&dinst=0& author=JOYCE+Mpercent2E+ROSENBERGpercent2C+AP+Business+Writer&title= Getting+the+Most+of+a+Trade+Show++&date=10percent2D17percent2D2002&query= trade+shows&maxdoc=30&idx=26 (accessed July 18, 2003).

publications. Involve your employees in show promotion and have them market the event through word-of-mouth. If possible, obtain a list of registered attendees and their contact information from the trade show organizers and include these individuals in your preshow promotions.

Be creative in your preshow promotions and work toward stimulating a desire to visit your exhibit. If you are having a drawing for a promotional product, send a picture of the product along with a registration form for the show attendees to bring to your booth. If hosting a game, send game tokens with your invitations. If you are providing rare novelty gifts to show participants, be sure to tell them before the show. And be sure to say that supplies are limited! Attendees will make an effort to find your booth early in the show to receive these novelty gifts. As a general rule, according to PPAI, promotional products of greater value generate more sales leads than products of lower value.

The next section features sample mailers designed to spark ideas for your preshow advertising. If possible, personalize your letters with prospect information.

Example One: New Product and Demonstration

Dear Friend,

We would like to invite you to an exciting event! Southwest Distributors will be participating in the Restaurant Trade Show June 10th from 8:00 AM to 4:00 PM at the City Civic Center. We will have the new **state-of-the-art meat slicer from P&G Manufacturers** on display along with other useful equipment for your kitchen. Additionally, we are hosting a **demonstration of P&G's new self-cleaning deep fryer** at **2:00** PM This is a must-see demonstration of a product that can simplify your operations and improve the efficiency of your kitchen staff!

Free to the first 50 visitors!

Be sure to visit the **Southwest Distributors** exhibit at Booth #15, check out the new products and get in on the outstanding **discounts for show attendees!** Plus, our **first 50 visitors** will receive a **free high-quality set of kitchen utensils!**

We look forward to seeing you there!

Sincerely,

Joe Smith, CEO

Example Two: Game Host Letter

Dear Friend,

We would like to invite you to an exciting event! Desert Beauty Supply will be participating in the *Beauty in a Bottle* trade show July 15th at the Southwest University Exhibition Hall from 8:00 AM to 4:00 PM. **The first 100 visitors to our booth will receive a FREE ROMANTIC GIFT SET!**

You will definitely want to stop by our exhibit at **booth #45** at 1:00 PM to play Beauty Queen Bingo for a chance to win a **Lambskin Leather Jacket from Sioux.** For your convenience, your game tokens are enclosed. Just bring them by the booth for your chance to win!

Join us in the fun! We look forward to seeing you there!

Sincerely,

Janet Roger, District Representative

Example Three: Drawing Letter

Dear Friend,

You are invited to the **Sports Extravaganza of the Year!** As participants in this trade show, Olympic Gym wants to make sure that your visit is a memorable one!

The newest line of **Workout Videos** will be on display at our booth and we will have a drawing for a **remote control boom box** to complement your workouts. For your convenience, your entry form is enclosed. Just drop it by at booth #94 and you will be entered to win! We will also be giving away **stopwatches** to all our booth visitors.

The Extravaganza will be held on May 15th at the Southside Gym from 8:00 AM to 4:00 PM. We look forward to seeing you there!

Sincerely,

Frank Jones, Lead Trainer

Example Four: Novelty Gift Letter

Dear Friend,

We are happy to invite your to the Sportsman Trade Show on October 15th at the Deerfield Shooting Range. The show will be held from 8:00 AM to 4:00 PM and will feature spectacular products, promotions, and competitions!

Be sure to stop by the Southside Sports exhibit at booth #23 to check out our newest supply of hunting and fishing equipment. At Southside Sports we are passionate about the fight against terrorism and we are certain that you want to "wipe out" terrorism as well. Therefore, we are giving away **free anti-terrorism toilet tissue** featuring the mug shot of Osama Bin Laden to all of our trade show visitors! Be sure to stop by and get yours while supplies last!

Join us and wipe out terrorism!

We look forward to seeing you at the event!

Sincerely,

Hefty Shindler, Owner, Southside Sports

Don't feel limited to traditional invitation letters to invite participants to the trade show. You can use formal invitations, one-page fliers, or innovative approaches such as sending a message in a bottle, on a silver platter, or in a real coconut.

Use creative invitations to encourage your prospects to attend the show and visit your booth.

Another excellent way to encourage attendance is to send half of a set of something with the other half retrieved at the show. For example, you can send one earring or one piece of a pen and pencil set along with an invitation inviting prospects to visit your booth to obtain the rest of the set.

Be sure to place an order for your printed supplies, literature, pens, pencils, and promotional products in plenty of time (generally six to eight weeks) to receive them before the show to guarantee availability. It is a catastrophe to promote a product to entice visitors and then be unable to deliver when they arrive at your booth. Before placing your orders, check with the event coordinators to obtain an estimated number of attendees. Order extra products to ensure that you don't run out in the middle of the show.

Staffing

Prepare your staff to work at the booth at the exhibit and ensure that you have adequate coverage so that booth visitors aren't left hanging or waiting long periods of time to talk to one of your representatives. Salespeople can engage more than one visitor at a time with product explanations and demonstrations, but it is a good idea to have several people who can also assist customers with placing orders. This ensures a private, one-on-one process.

Select outgoing, friendly, and knowledgeable staff members to work at your booth. Train them to engage exhibit visitors in conversation, to introduce them to your products and services, and to promote the positive and beneficial aspects of your offerings. At the show, encourage your workers to walk around and look at the other booths to give them important insight into similar businesses in your industry. However, make sure that your booth has sufficient coverage at all times during the show.

Set up a mock booth and hold a rehearsal before the show. Make sure that your plan is sound, your booth is attractive, and your staff is prepared to answer any questions that may arise during presentations. Brainstorm with your staff to determine what challenges you may face at the show and to ensure that you are prepared in terms of knowledge, products, literature, and supplies.

If you intend to have a display such as a television and VCR or special lighting, make sure that your booth has the necessary power outlets to accommodate your needs.

Supplies

Here is a basic checklist of items you may need at the show:

- ☐ Literature
- ☐ Catalogs
- ☐ Business cards
- ☐ Sample products
- ☐ Promotional products

- ☐ Decorations
- ☐ Signs
- ☐ Sales slips
- ☐ Credit card slips
- ☐ Order forms
- ☐ Price tags
- ☐ Index cards
- ☐ Clip boards
- ☐ Ink pens
- ☐ Pencils
- ☐ Markers
- ☐ Note pads
- ☐ Sacks, bags or boxes
- ☐ Collection boxes and entry forms for drawings or contests
- ☐ Game pieces for games
- ☐ Prizes
- ☐ Tape
- ☐ Scissors
- ☐ Wire cutters
- ☐ Wire
- ☐ Stapler and staples
- ☐ Stick pins or thumbtacks
- ☐ Rubber bands
- ☐ Table cloths
- ☐ Display racks
- ☐ Cork boards
- ☐ Basic tool kit
- ☐ Calculator
- ☐ Change box or pouch for onsite sales
- ☐ Bottled water
- ☐ Headache and allergy medicine

Go over this list before the show and add anything else you can think of that you might need. Being prepared will help the show to run smoothly and will minimize the stress that can be associated with such an event.

At the Show

Arrive early in order to prepare your booth and give yourself time for last-minute trips to the store in case you forgot something. Check with event organizers to find the earliest time you can set up your booth. If permitted, it is ideal to complete most of the set up the evening before the show, leaving the products and literature in their proper placement for the morning of the show. If other displays are already set up, walk around and look at them. How does your exhibit compare?

After you have your booth prepared, step back and look at it from an attendee's perspective and make sure that it is visually attractive and well-organized. Ask yourself:

- Is it immediately clear what your company does or sells?
- Are your items for sale clearly marked and priced?
- Is your literature readily available for visitors to pick up?
- Have you strategically placed your giveaway products so that attendees are first exposed to your products, services, and literature before retrieving giveaways?
- Is the path clear for visitors to approach your displays?
- Are some of your products displayed at eye level where they will catch the attention of passersby?
- Are your promotions clearly visible?
- Does your booth display items of interest?
- Is your image effectively portrayed?
- How does your exhibit measure up to the others?
- Do you have a comfortable area for sales staff to assist customers with purchases?
- Is your sales area organized?

Once you are sure that your booth is in order, take a deep breath and relax before the crowd arrives. Take time to check out the other booths and visit with exhibitors. Look for exhibitors with whom you can network and who may provide you with resources or complementary alliances. Be sure that your staff is prepared to greet visitors before they begin to arrive.

Show Time!

Greet each visitor with a smile, a friendly "hello," and an introduction. Invite them to take literature and giveaways from your booth. Engage them in conversation as much as possible. Learn about their needs and make sure they know what you have to offer. Provide product demonstrations and answer questions. Make sure they know if they can place orders or purchase products onsite and guide them through the process. Thank visitors for stopping by your booth.

Be aware of your body language and your posture. Never sit down in the booth unless you are meeting one-on-one with a customer or prospect. Be open, friendly, and helpful. Remain positive and don't get discouraged if the volume of traffic does not meet your expectations. If the traffic at your booth is not sufficient, don't be afraid to walk out on the floor and invite people to your display. Don't overload them with information but instead chat with them and explain solutions that your company can provide that meet their needs. Ask open-ended questions that require more than a "yes," "no," or "fine" answer. Use light and appropriate humor in discussions. If you have a drawing or contest, encourage attendees to sign up. If you don't, collect business cards and contact information from the patrons.

Take brief breaks as needed so that you don't wear out. Slow down, stretch, and refresh yourself before going back on the floor. Working a trade show can be exhausting and overwhelming. These breaks are important to the effectiveness of your presentation.

After the Show

Be sure to follow up immediately with new contacts and current customers following the show. Send a thank-you card or note along with an imprinted promotional product, a business card, and a full catalog of your products to people who visited your booth. Add your new contacts to your customer database to be included in sequential mailings so you can continue to market to them and invite them to your next show. Make sales calls to individuals who expressed an interest in a certain product or service at the show. For an extra networking boost, consider hosting a cocktail party after the event to give you the opportunity to meet with prospects in a more relaxed environment.

Meet with your staff after the show to evaluate the experience. What worked? What didn't work? What can you do better to improve your next show? View each experience, whether positive or negative, as a learning experience. The staff that worked the show possesses valuable knowledge, experience, and ideas. Put that expertise and innovation to work to make each show you participate in better than the last!

5

Sales Promotion

As we've discussed earlier, two ways to increase sales are to increase customer base and to increase the per-transaction expenditures of current customers. Sales promotions can be used to attract new customers or to keep customers loyal to your business. This is critical because your competition is constantly trying to woo customers away from you so that they can add them to their own customer base. Competition in attracting new customers is intense regardless of your industry.

Remember that the cost of attracting new customers is much more than retaining your existing customer base. Sales promotions give you an opportunity to stay in touch with your existing customers while providing them with incentives to continue buying from you. If you are interested in keeping the customers you have, sales promotions will keep customers interested and motivated to buy.

Sales promotions are programs that add an incentive that is intended to stimulate purchases. They are effective in encouraging initial purchases from prospects, increasing the amount of a purchase, and rewarding repeat purchases that in turn encourages return customers and reorders. Historically, service companies rarely used sales promotions. They were primarily utilized for the sale of products; however, service companies are realizing the benefits of sales promotions as well and are beginning to maximize the power of the promotions. Service companies are highly reliant on repeat business, so rewarding loyal customers is a logical approach to retaining their business.

The basic steps in developing a sales promotion include:

1. Setting objectives
2. Determining the duration of the promotion
3. Selecting strategies
4. Developing specific tactics to meet the objectives
5. Putting the promotion into action

Setting Objectives

In planning a sales promotion, start by setting your objectives. Clear and measurable objectives will help you to plan a promotion that gets results. What exactly do you intend to accomplish through the sales promotion? Some sample objectives include:

- Increase sales volume.
- Deplete the inventory of a discontinued item.
- Reward and retain current customers.
- Encourage repurchases.
- Attract first-time buyers.
- Increase the customer base.
- Encourage initial sales on a new product.

Duration

Sales promotions should have a set duration. The purpose of setting a period of duration is two-fold. First, it keeps a sales promotion from becoming stale. Many marketing professionals make the mistake of developing a unique and effective sales promotion and solely relying on it for an extended period of time. Regardless of how fantastic a promotion is, it will become stagnant over time. For example, offering a free travel bag with purchases over $50 is an excellent incentive for customers to make initial purchases. However, if you run the exact promotion for an extended period, it can actually discourage repeat business. Customers only need or desire a certain number of travel bags and after they have them, they will seek promotions that are fresh and new. Therefore, the first purpose of setting a time limit on a promotion is that it introduces new, innovative promotions to keep customers coming back for more.

The second reason for establishing a promotion's duration is to give prospects a sense of urgency to make a purchase. If your sales promotion tells prospects that they will receive an incentive for placing an order, they may say, "Oh, I need to keep this information." On the other hand, if your sales promotion tells them that they will receive a certain incentive if they place an order by a specific date, they are more inclined to immediately pick up the phone and place the order. This tactic takes advantage of the human tendency to buy on impulse. Many people buy on impulse. Deadline dates for special offers often ignite the impulse, resulting in immediate action. This immediate action is exactly what you need to make a sales promotion successful.

Selecting Strategies

Selecting strategies for your sales promotions can be a bit challenging. Development of effective strategies requires some innovation and creative talent, but it doesn't require a rocket scientist. The best approach is to brainstorm for ideas, select the ones that are most attractive, and try them. Always track and evaluate the results of each sales promotion to see what works and what doesn't. The knowledge gleaned from such activities is priceless. It enables you to create new approaches, similar to the most effective ones and to ditch strategies that don't produce desirable results. The final outcome is an arsenal of sales promotion strategies that work.

Sales promotion strategy is how you communicate your program to your prospects or "promote the promotion." Every representative from the CEO to the store clerk should be informed of sales promotions and promoting them should be a part of everyday operations. Certainly, you will advertise your sales promotions; however, communicating them verbally, one-on-one, to existing customers, browsers, associates, and other contacts is an excellent tactic to make your sales promotions known. For example, a restaurant may run a sales promotion to introduce a new menu item, such as after-dinner coffees. While at a Chamber of Commerce meeting, the CEO could say, "By the way, we have some new after-dinner coffees that are exceptional and when you order one, you receive a free crystal coffee mug." Some of those contacts might just stop by for coffee and have dinner while they are there. The purchasing agent may mention the promotion in a similar manner to the paper goods salesperson, beef salesperson, produce salesperson, and so on. Meanwhile, the bookkeeper is mentioning it to the accountant, the banker, and the clerks at the post office. Of course, the hostesses and waitstaff are promoting it in the dining room. As you can see, by getting all members of your staff involved in the sales promotion process, the effects and the results are multiplied.

Your promotions can be announced in your current catalog, in direct-mail fliers, newsletters, e-mail marketing messages, and fax broadcasts. Fliers can be placed in mail order shipments, in the bag with retail purchases, or sent as statement stuffers. In-store signage on doors, counters, or even hung from ceilings is also effective. Printing your current promotions on your invoices is also a great idea. Media advertisements in the newspaper, magazines, and trade publications will get the word out as will radio advertising. Of course, your budget and target market will dictate your strategy. It is important to establish a healthy balance of strategies for promoting your promotions.

Developing Tactics to Meet Objectives

Notice that developing your tactics for your sales promotion is dependent on the objectives. To realize the results you desire, tactics must be based on the objectives you have set. Your tactics involve the specific promotional programs you will employ to fulfill your sales promotion objectives. For instance, if your goal is to deplete the inventory of a certain product, you will offer incentives with the purchase of that particular product. A promotion that provides incentives for purchases in general may increase those sales, but is not targeted to accomplish the specific objective.

There are a number of objectives that can be achieved through a successful sales promotion. The effectiveness of the promotion in meeting those objectives is directly linked to alignment of the promotion with the purpose. If you proactively pursue the goals and objectives set for your sales promotion program, the results can be astounding.

Here are some examples of tactics aligned with objectives:

Objectives	Tactics
Increase sales volume	Promotional product incentives for placing an order that meets a set dollar amount

Deplete inventory of a discontinued item	A free promotional product with the purchase of the specific item
Reward and retain current customers	A customer appreciation program including a letter of appreciation and a free promotional product or an offer of a promotional product with the next order
Encourage repurchases	An offer of a free promotional product with the next order
Attract first-time buyers	A first-time buyer's promotion that offers a free promotional product with a customer's initial order
Increase the customer base	A first-time buyer's program or a referral program that rewards current customers and/or employees with a free promotional product when one of their referrals makes a first-time purchase
Encourage initial sales on a new product or service	A free promotional product with the purchase of the new product or service and/or free promotional products as a reward in an employee sales competition

Putting the Promotion into Action

Once you have set the objectives for your sales promotion, determined your strategies, determined the duration of the promotion, and developed specific tactics to meet the objectives, you are ready to put your plan into action and begin your promotion.

First, you need to decide what promotional products you will offer that will be appealing to prospects and encourage them to react to your promotion. There are a few things to consider when selecting your promotional products, such as:

- Characteristics of the target market
- Promotional incentives offered by your competitors
- Costs and benefits
- Association between the promotion, objective, and promotional product

The use of promotional products in sales promotions differs greatly from the use of promotional products in advertising. In advertising, the purpose is to get your name in front of prospects so that they will remember you, to increase name and brand recognition, and to provide easy access to your contact information. Providing imprinted promotional products is an excellent strategy to fulfill the purpose of advertising; however, sales promotions require something that provides value to the customer. If you can combine an imprinted item with a valuable item, such as offering imprinted calendars at year-end, that is certainly a viable option. However, generally speaking, it is better to offer items that benefit the receiver rather than those products that serve solely to advertise.

Characteristics of the Target Market

Knowing your target market will enable you to select promotional product incentives that will prompt them to buy. Chances are, if your target market consists of senior citizens, they will not be inspired by an offer to receive a free video game with their purchase. Alternatively, a target audience of teenagers may love the free video game offer, but will not respond to a CD of classical music.

A target market consisting primarily of women may be prompted to purchase if your promotional product incentive is an aromatherapy gift set, but men may be more impressed with golf or barbecue accessories. A briefcase may catch the eye of a business professional, while a piece of luggage would be more attractive to the general adult population and a backpack appeals to a college or high-school student. Children are inspired by stuffed animals and toys and pressure their parents to buy something in order to get a "free" plaything. Take care to select promotional product incentives that will create desire for your specific audience.

To help you develop ideas for specific types of target audiences, look over the following compilation that contains an array of suggestive samples that have been put together to prompt your imagination and spark your creative ability to devise the perfect plan for your sales promotions. If your specific needs aren't addressed by these samples, you may wish to browse through a promotional products catalog. See our Resource Guide at the end of this book to discover the immense options that can make your sales promotion original and effective.

Ideas for New Parents
- Bibs
- Gift baskets

- Bottles
- Banks
- Diaper bag
- Clothing
- Photo albums and journals
- Bath products

Ideas for a General Male Audience

- Binoculars
- Baseball caps
- Apparel
- Passport holder
- Tool kits
- Barbecue sets
- Barbecue
- Coolers
- Pocket watch
- Stadium seat
- Jewelry
- Electronics
- Timepieces

Ideas for a General Female Audience

- Gift baskets
- Sweets
- Totes
- Jewelry
- First aid kits
- Clothing
- Jewelry box
- Electronics Business card holders
- Computer cases

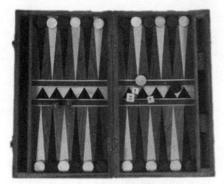

Ideas for Children

- Toys
- Water guns
- Sport balls and items
- Baby blocks
- Stuffed animals
- Etch-A-Sketch
- Frisbees
- Dress-up and costume items
- Paddle balls
- Art sets
- Inflatable toys
- Traditional toys
- Science and discovery items
- Bath toys
- Toy cars

Ideas for Teenagers

- Collectibles
- Bandanas
- Sunglasses
- Electronics
- Calculators
- Cameras
- Baseball caps
- Stadium seats
- CD holders
- Games
- Car emergency kits
- Personal grooming kits
- Apparel
- Beach chairs
- Swimwear
- Stress relievers

- Backpacks
- Spa items

Ideas for College Students

- Watches
- Calendars and planners
- Electronics
- Computer accessories
- Computer cases/totes
- Calculators
- Dictionaries and thesauruses
- Inspirational books
- Desk sets
- Barbecues
- Telescopes
- Cameras
- Baseball caps
- Stadium seats
- CDs and CD holders
- Games
- Car emergency kits
- Personal grooming kits
- Apparel
- Beach chairs
- Swimwear
- Stress relievers
- Backpacks
- Spa items

Ideas for Athletes and Sports Fans

- Duffels and totes
- Sporting equipment
- Athletic apparel
- Specialty items

- Outdoor sporting goods
- Totes
- Sport seating
- Coolers
- Exercise equipment
- Pedometers
- Water bottles
- Stadium seats
- Stopwatches
- First aid kits

Ideas for the Outdoorsman
- Weather gear
- First aid kit
- Seating
- Coolers
- Flashlights
- Barbecues and smokers
- Hammock
- First aid kit
- Outdoor knives
- Lanterns
- Travel kits
- Utility tools
- Camping equipment
- Snow sporting goods
- Fishing gear and tackle

Ideas for the Business Professional
- Timepieces
- Calendars
- Calculators
- Totes and computer bags
- Desk sets

- Travel items
- Desk clocks
- Jewelry
- Planners
- Stress relievers
- Awards

Your Competitors' Promotional Incentives

In deciding what promotional products
to use for your sales promotion, you need to check out your competition
and see what they are doing. If the competitors are offering first-time
buyers a full set of luggage as an incentive for their first order, providing
a piece of luggage as an initial order incentive will not be appealing.
There are several different methods you can employ to differentiate
your sales promotion from your competitors to make it more appealing
to your audience. You can offer a promotional product that is similar,
but better than your competitors. The following table depicts this
competition:

Competitor's Promotional Product	Your Promotional Product
A piece of luggage	A set of luggage
A headset radio	A portable stereo
An outdoor grill	An outdoor grill with utensils
A vinyl briefcase	A leather briefcase
A portable television	A full-size television
A sports jacket	A full workout suit
A box of golf balls	A golf bag filled with golf balls
A bicycle repair kit	A bicycle
A calendar book	A leather bound planner book
A watch	A desk clock
A calculator	An electronic data bank
A magazine	A book
A stadium cushion	A portable stadium chair

Another approach is to offer something entirely different, for example:

Competitor's Promotional Product	Your Promotional Product
A piece of luggage	A portable stereo
A headset radio	An outdoor grill
An outdoor grill	A folding chair
A vinyl briefcase	A computer repair kit
A portable television	A leather jacket
A sports jacket	A golf bag
A box of golf balls	A sports jacket
A bicycle repair kit	A family game set
A calendar book	A desktop organizer
A watch	A ring
A calculator	A briefcase
A magazine	A photo album
A stadium cushion	An ice chest or beverage cooler

Novelty gifts that are unusual and hard to find are also a great promotional product incentive for your sales promotions. Personalized items like playing cards with a custom picture are great promotional incentives.

Cost versus Benefits

Another consideration in selecting your promotional product incentive items is the cost and the benefits that use of the products will bring. Many people have difficulty realizing the power of promotional products and view them as an unnecessary expense. To many, it just doesn't make sense to give a first-time buyer a promotional product valued at $20 for an initial order of $50. However, when you view this scenario in a different light, you'll see that promotional products portray goodwill that encourages repeat business and strong, loyal customer relationships. Studies show that customers who received promotional product incentives are more dedicated and produce a greater volume of sales than those who don't receive anything. So looking at things in that light, what is the benefit compared to the cost of a promotional product incentive?

Developing Goodwill

A 1992 study by PPAI showed that promotional products foster positive attitudes and feelings toward a company that provides the products to their customers. A textbook publisher was the feature of a study in which 4,000 educators were sent a letter with a pocket calculator, a letter with a highlighter pen, or only a letter. The customers who received the promotional products expressed more goodwill toward the company and its salespeople. Those who received the calculator were more positive than the rest. The customers who received the calculator rated the sales representatives' proficiency 34 percent higher than those who didn't receive a promotional product and the ones who received the highlighter rated proficiency and ability 16 percent higher than those who received only a letter. When asked about personal feelings toward the company and its representatives, customers who received the calculator rated the company 52 percent higher than those who received only a letter.[1]

Increasing Response Rates and Expenditure

As discussed earlier, studies prove that promotional products and promotional product incentives used in advertising and sales promotions increase response rates. A PPAI study indicated that customers who receive promotional products return sooner and order more frequently than customers who do not receive promotional products. Reorders occurred 18 percent sooner with the use of promotional products. A separate study showed that over an eight-month period, first-time buyers who received promotional products spent 27 percent more than those who received coupons and 139 percent more than those that just received a letter and those who received promotional products were 75 percent more likely to patronize the business over the period of the study. Therefore, new customers who received

---

[1]Promotional Products Association International, "Build Customer Goodwill with Promotional Products" (2003), www.ppai.com/ProductsResources/Research/SalesPower Tools/SPT_CustomerGoodwill.asp (accessed July 27, 2003).

promotional products as an incentive spent more and were more regular customers than those who did not receive the promotional products.[2]

The bottom line? The results of these demonstrate that promotional products are extremely effective in attracting customers, increasing average sales, encouraging repeat purchases, and retaining loyal customers. Considering all of those factors, what is the benefit of providing a promotional product in your sales promotions? How does that compare to the cost of the product? Take a good look at the results and you will find that the cost of promotional products is well worth the benefits they produce.

Promotion, Objective, and Promotional Product

The final consideration in selecting specific promotional products for your sales promotion campaign is the association between the promotion, the objective, and the promotional product. By now you are familiar with the concept of setting objectives and developing a plan for promotion that is aligned with the objective.

If at all possible, it is a good idea to provide a free promotional product or promotional product incentive that complements the products or services you are attempting to promote or suits the needs of the target audience. For example, if you are promoting the sale of books, a book bag would be a logical choice for a promotional product incentive. On the other hand, if you are promoting the sale of book bags, a free book with the purchase of the bag would be complementary. When selling CD players, a free CD or CD case would be an incentive to buy a CD player. As discussed earlier, always make sure that your promotional product incentives are appealing to the target audience. Conduct informal or formal surveys of your customers to discover their interests, desires, and needs.

Types of Sales Promotions

Sales promotions using promotional products are common and effective for a number of different types of promotions. The communication of these promotions can be accomplished in a variety ways including

---

[2]Promotional Products Association International, "Keep Customers Coming Back with Promotional Products" (2003), www.ppai.com/ProductsResources/Research/SalesPower Tools/SPT_RepeatBusiness.asp (accessed July 27, 2003).

word-of-mouth promotion, media advertising, e-mail and newsletter advertising, print advertising, and cold calling. Catalogs, brochures, and invoices can have banners announcing the sales promotions. One of the most common methods of promoting a sales promotion is direct mail or e-mail marketing; therefore, we have provided specific examples of such marketing to help you create your own outstanding sales promotion campaigns.

Promotion to Increase Sales Volume

Dear Customer,

We have an awesome promotion in effect from now until August 31 that you just have to get in on! During this period, every customer who places an order of $150 or more will be rewarded with a state-of-the-art handheld electronic game.

If you've had your eye on a new game console or a couple of video games, now is the time to order! Not only will you receive the products you've been dreaming about, you'll also get a free handheld electronic game to keep you entertained on those long trips or boring periods of time when you are unable to use your game console.

Order now and claim your **FREE electronic game!**

Sincerely,

John Hanks, Video Game Enthusiast

Promotion to Deplete an Inventory Item

Dear Friend,

We are clearing out our inventory of Lane sofas to make room for some new designs. We want to give our best customers the first opportunity to take advantage of the once-in-a-lifetime prices on these top-of-the-line sofas. So, in addition to our remarkably low prices on the clearance items, you will receive a **free furniture vacuum** with your purchase.

(Continued)

This promotion begins this Saturday and will run until all of the clearance sofas are gone. They will go fast, so be sure to stop by early to select your choice sofa and claim your free vacuum!

See you Saturday!

Roland Warren, Best Choice Furniture

Promotion to Reward and Retain Current Customers

Dear Friend,

We would like to take this opportunity to tell our dedicated customers "Thank You!" You are invited to our Customer Appreciation Day celebration on Friday, April 15th from 8:00 AM to 4:00 PM. We will be serving refreshments all day and when you present this letter, you will receive a **Free Mantel Clock** as a token of our friendship and appreciation for your devotion Cook's Home Depot.

Stop by to visit, enjoy refreshments, check out our new inventory and collect your free gift as an expression of our gratitude!

Sincerely,

Fred Cook, Cook's Home Depot

To Encourage Repurchases

Dear Friend,

Thank you for the recent order you placed with Henderson's Vitamin Center. We are certain that you will enjoy your products and will be eager to replenish your supply in 30 days! To express our appreciation of your continued business, we would like to give you a **free Fitness and Exercise Pocket Guide** with your next order.

When you make another purchase before April 30, we will automatically send you this helpful guide. We look forward to seeing you soon!

Sincerely,

Amber Rollins, Health and Fitness Trainer

First-Time Buyer Promotion

Dear Fellow Chef:

At American Chef Supply, we understand that high-quality equipment and cookware is essential to your profession. Through collaboration with professional chefs all over the world we have developed the most functional cookware products available in the industry today. Enclosed you will find a catalog that showcases our most popular and highly demanded items.

As an expression of appreciation and to welcome you into our base of highly satisfied customers, we are proud to send you a **free set of utensils** with your first order from our comprehensive catalog. Act quickly as these exclusive gifts are available only while supplies last! We look forward to serving your every need.

Sincerely,

David Knight, Gourmet Chef and CEO

Promotion to Increase Customer Base

Dear Friend,

The Family Fun Club is a positive place for families to gather for entertainment and to enjoy activities such as games, movies, swimming, dinners and dances in an atmosphere designed to help build strong family ties. Additionally, members receive special rates on our banquet facilities for those special occasions that are so dear to the heart. The membership fee for a family is only $55 per year and for a limited time; we are giving each new family a **Free Family Game Set** when they apply for membership to the Club.

We look forward to having your family become part of our family! Come by and sign your family up for the many benefits provided by membership to The Family Fun Club and claim your free family game set. Hurry while supplies last!

Sincerely,

Art Brown, Director

Promotion to Introduce a New Product or Service

Dear Friend,

   Hanna's Car Wash is proud to announce our new full detail services. Bring your car by for a full detail before the end of the month and you will receive a **FREE PORTABLE AIR COMPRESSOR!**

   We look forward to seeing you and we are certain you will be pleased with our full-detail services!

   Sincerely,

   Bill Hanna, Owner

Reward the Promoters of the Promotion

Earlier we discussed how sales promotion efforts can be multiplied when your entire staff participates in marketing a sales promotion. In addition to your staff, you can also commission your customers or other organizations to help with your promotion. Without a doubt, they will have a "What's in it for me?" agenda. The following explores ways to bring your current customers into your own outside salesforce, multiplying your sales promotion efforts.

   To promote your program, distribute coupon-like referral slips to current customers. When a new customer brings in the referral slip, the referring customer is entered into a competition or drawing for a high-dollar promotional product. The reward in a competition would go to the individual who generated the most responses or the slips can be dropped into a drawing box for an opportunity to win the promotional product. Employees, customers, and organizations can all participate in these types of promotions. Of course, the promotional product that you offer should be desirable to whomever your competitors are to encourage participation. For example:

- Telescopes
- Game tables
- Binoculars
- Televisions
- Outdoor shade canopies

- Stereo sets
- Electronics
- Coolers
- Cameras
- Tools
- Apparel

Use promotional products to multiply your sales promotion efforts.

6

Public Relations

What is public relations anyway? There are many definitions of public relations, but the most commonly accepted is the definition provided by the Public Relations Society of America: "Public relations helps an organization and its publics adapt mutually to each other."[1] So, in practice, public relations is the process of adapting to your community and/or marketplace and gaining acceptance from it. Essentially, public relations is all activities that a business or organization engages in to "fit in" with its community or marketplace. Public relations efforts bring an organization and its publics into harmony through the development of mutually beneficial relationships.

To achieve positive public relations, it is critical that an organization understands the attitudes and values of the public and establishes acceptable policies and practices to foster constructive relationships and a healthy perception in the public eye. The process encompasses anticipating, analyzing, and reacting to public opinion, issues, and attitudes. This reaction may include taking responsibility for your social and citizenship responsibilities; communicating your role in the community or your stand on issues; marketing; fund-raising; employee, community, and government relations; and support of issues that are important to the public.

The benefit of positive public relations is that your company becomes known as a company that "cares." Your commitment to the

---

[1] Public Relations Society of America, *Official PRSA Definition*, www.prsa.org/_Resources/Profession/index.asp?ident=prof1/(accessed July 30, 2003).

public increases the public's commitment to you, your business, and the purchase of your products and services. Public relations give you and your workforce a positive attitude and a feeling of team and community spirit. It helps you attract good employees. When the whole staff is involved in public relations, it eliminates corporate isolation and develops new contacts and associates.

When you begin a public relations campaign, you need to clearly define what you are trying to accomplish. Who are your publics? What is important to them? Be sure to include your employees, prospective employees, your community, and your marketplace in your planning. Some broad categories of public concern include children, education, political matters, poverty, disease, environment, crime, and other social issues. Addressing and supporting these areas of public concern paves the way for positive public relations.

While public relations can involve the use of professional firms or consultants who specialize in generating news and goodwill for their clients, businesses can develop their own campaigns with a personal, grass-roots approach.

Promotional Products and Public Relations

Promotional products can boost public relations. Doing a good deed makes you feel good, but letting everyone know you are behind the good deed attracts business *and* makes you feel good. You don't have to blow your own horn and run newspaper or radio advertisements that say "Look what we did." There are a number of ways to support your public's interests and get your name out in the process. Promotional products give you the edge to accomplish this mission.

The American Institute of Philanthropy (see Resource Guide at the end of the book) publishes a categorized list of charity organizations. This watch-dog organization's mission is to assist donors in making informed decisions. Additionally, the databases of the National Center for Charitable Statistics (see Resource Guide) are a great source for collecting information on nonprofit and charitable organizations. Organizations such as Charity America (see Resource Guide) have adopt-a-project programs which individual organizations and communities can support through fund-raising efforts.

Communities often have nonprofit organizations that promote a cause that is important to the local area. Whether it is to preserve local historical sites, enhance education in the arts, preserve open space, or build new sports fields for local children, the support of these organizations is an excellent public relations move. Support can be provided through financial contributions, donation of needed supplies, and volunteer services.

Public Relations Programs

The following section explores some ideas for supporting your public's areas of concern. However, your community's needs are as unique as its residents. Be creative in developing your public relations program and address issues that are dear to the hearts of those in your marketplace.

If a lack of registered voters is of concern in your market area, support voter registration efforts by providing needed supplies and imprinted promotional products to be used in the registration booths.

Provide needed supplies to promote public interests.

Many communities support organizations, such as the United Way, that provide support to their local area. The United Way of America is the nation's leader in providing community solutions.

Approximately 1,400 community-based organizations are independent, separately incorporated, and governed by local volunteers. The focus of the United Way is to bring communities together to make a difference by addressing the needs of the community. The United Way and similar organizations generally have an annual drive to raise money for the year. Many businesses find it beneficial to support these organizations and employees are very apt to provide support and volunteer services to such locally driven organizations.

By getting employees involved in benefit drives through volunteer services and corporate payroll deductions for pledges, an organization can multiply its contributions to organizations that generally provide a lot of publicity for contributors. Although employees often contribute to causes important to them, employers can encourage contributions through offering promotional products. All employees who make a contribution can receive an incentive gift or you can separate your employees into teams and provide prizes for the team with the greatest contributions.

> Multiply your contributions by rewarding your employees for theirs.

There are a number of national campaigns that your organization can support to demonstrate interest in the greater good of our country. The American Cancer Society Relay for Life (see Resource Guide) enables communities to come together in the fight against cancer. The 24-hour event features team solicitation of sponsorship donations and fund-raisers. Making Strides Against Breast Cancer is another similar event that benefits the American Cancer Society.

Jump Rope for Heart and Hoops for Heart are educational fund-raising events for the American Heart Association that are held in thousands of elementary schools nationwide. These events raise funds for medical research and programs such as HeartPower! that help to prevent heart disease and stroke. The events also provide health education for youth and build character by getting them involved in community services. The American Heart Walk is similar to the American Cancer Society's Relay for Life. (See the Resource Guide for more information.)

The HIV and AIDS pandemics are a tremendous threat to the continuance of entire civilizations in many countries and the search for a cure is of public interest worldwide. According to the AIDS Research Alliance of America, nearly 40 million people are currently living with the HIV virus. In 2005, 2.8 million lives were lost to AIDS and the disease has orphaned more than 13 million children worldwide. In Africa, there are entire communities made up of AIDS orphans. A number of organizations are joining in the fight against AIDS by providing education regarding prevention, research for a cure, and treatment in addition to educating the vast number of AIDS orphans who have been left to take care of themselves. The AIDS Research Alliance of America's Ride for Research is usually a two-day bike ride fund-raiser that supports AIDS research.

The American Red Cross holds blood drives to ensure that America's blood banks don't run dry in times of need. According to the American Red Cross, convenience is a driving force for people donating blood. In fact, 85 percent of donations made through the Red Cross occur at sponsored drives rather than through donor centers. Sponsoring a corporate or community blood drive is a healthy public relations effort. To encourage community participation (and bring people into your place of business), you can hold a drawing for a promotional product door prize. You can also provide imprinted water bottles, t-shirts, or stress balls with your company name and a message such as "I gave blood" or "We support the Red Cross." (To learn more, see our Resource Guide.)

- Support national events that assist with social and health issues.
- Hold a drawing for a promotional product door prize to improve blood drive recruitment results.
- Get your name out to participants in sponsored blood drives.

As you can see, there are a number of national organizations that provide fund-raising opportunities to address issues of public concern. The ones listed are just a handful of examples. Supporting events and projects such as these help to solve or minimize the impact of social issues and are outstanding public relations opportunities. You can get involved by sponsoring events or encouraging your employees and community to participate in fund-raisers. Providing imprinted water bottles, visors, sunscreen, rest stations, and participation prizes can help with the event and get your organization's name associated with the effort.

Prizes promote competitive participation.

If your community could benefit from a little sprucing up, organize and sponsor a "Clean Community" drive. For this type of endeavor, organizations join forces to recruit volunteers to adopt a park, neighborhood, school, street, or highway. To promote the event, you may provide first-, second-, and third-place promotional product prizes to the group recruiting the most volunteers. During registration and recruiting efforts, you may supply automobile litter bags that feature a tear-off coupon for your company. In addition to supporting the clean-up effort beyond the event, this inspires goodwill for your company in the eyes of the community. Of course, if your employees participate as a work group, be sure that they wear apparel imprinted with your company logo for added exposure. Clean community drives provide outstanding exposure for the sponsoring organization and directly address a problem of public concern.

Use coupon imprinted litter bags to recruit volunteers and attract traffic to your business.

Poverty is another concern throughout America. Many communities have community (or soup) kitchens that provide healthy meals for poverty-stricken individuals and families. Community kitchens need support to help fight hunger. This support can be provided through volunteerism, financial or product contributions, fund-raisers, or needed supplies. Organizing volunteer groups and other support efforts, especially during the holiday season, can be particularly rewarding for all involved.

> Provide imprinted aprons to demonstrate your support of community efforts to curb hunger.

Many communities offer homeless shelters for homeless individuals and families. These shelters are appreciative of any assistance that supports their efforts including imprinted blankets, toiletry items, sleeping bags, clothing, and so on.

> Help with sheltering efforts for the homeless.

Another worthy organization is Habitat for Humanity International that is dedicated to providing affordable housing and assistance to those in need by building homes. The organization enables families to purchase the homes they have helped to build at cost and with a zero-interest mortgage. The projects are supported by contributions of money, supplies, and volunteer services. You can encourage your employees to get involved in a Habitat for Humanity project by rewarding their efforts with promotional products for contributing a specified number of hours to a project. Of course, you will want your workers to be adorned with your company name and logo when working on housing projects.

> Reward volunteerism with promotional product gifts.
>
> *   *   *
>
> Adorn your workers with your company name and logo.

Child and adult literacy and vocational programs improve the quality of life for many people. Such programs can be supported through donations, program sponsorship, supplies, and volunteerism. The offering of promotional product incentives can encourage participation and also motivate participants to excel in the program.

Show you care by providing needed items to literacy and vocational programs.

✳   ✳   ✳

Encourage participation by providing incentives.

✳   ✳   ✳

Encourage achievement by recognizing and rewarding accomplishments.

✳   ✳   ✳

Acknowledge and reward volunteer efforts of your employees in the community.

Veterans' organizations often raise money to support interests of veterans who have served our country sacrificing for our freedom. Efforts for veterans can be supported by providing items to be sold in fund-raisers or given to contributors in appreciation of their support.

Support fund-raising efforts for veterans' causes.

Safety education of children is another area of concern for most communities. Some communities hold events to teach bike, personal and fire safety. Your participation can be enhanced by providing incentives such as gifts for participants and door prize drawings.

Promote child safety events by providing gifts and gift bags.

✳   ✳   ✳

Encourage participation with door prizes.

To support youth organizations such as the Boy or Girl Scouts, Boys and Girls Clubs, and Little League in addition to school music programs, school competitions, travel, and more, you can provide items for the groups to raffle or auction. This is often much more profitable than a cash donation. Providing a raffle item in addition to sponsoring the printing of the raffle tickets will enable you to imprint your company information on tickets that will be distributed throughout the community.

Support your youth by sponsoring a raffle.

*   *   *

Sponsor sports events by providing your printed cups to be used in concession stands.

Local athletic groups and leagues can be helped through the donation of items such as antenna balls, stadium cushions, or coffee mugs that can be sold as team, school, or league fund-raisers. You can also provide supplies such as printed cups to be used in concession stands at games. These approaches help the athletic groups and depict your organization in a positive way.

Provide fund-raising items for athletic groups.

Schools often have educational programs and celebrations related to nationally recognized events such as Read Across America, National Walk to School Day, Red Ribbon Week, African American History Month, and more. Other helpful programs are gang and drug prevention programs and programs that promote youth development such as D.A.R.E. and Character Counts. Supporting these initiatives are good for your community, its children and your company.

Provide assistance to youth education and character building programs.

Sample Press Releases

Joe's Restaurant Hosts New Year's Eve Extravaganza

FOR IMMEDIATE RELEASE   CONTACT: Joe Doe
(555) 123-4567
joe@joesrestaurant.com

Anytown, State: Joe's Restaurant is now accepting reservations for its New Year's Eve Extravaganza. Guests will delight in live music performed by Wally and the Wailers, an extensive buffet dinner created by Chef John Simms, champagne toasts, festive decorations and unique party favors. The adults-only event is priced at $55 per person and reservations are required. The evening will feature one seating at 8:00 PM. Cocktails and dancing begin at 7:00 PM. For more information, call Joe's Restaurant at (555) 123-4567. Joe's is located at 1234 Any Street in Anytown.

Joe's Restaurant's third-annual New Year's Eve Extravaganza is always the highlight of the holiday season for regular and first-time customers. "I wouldn't spend my New Year's Eve anywhere else," says Patrick Roy of Anytown. "The music, the dancing, the food—it's the highlight of my holiday season."

A 100-foot buffet will feature holiday favorites including prime rib, roast turkey, mashed potatoes, and Yorkshire pudding. Chef John Simms takes special pride in this event's delicacies. "New Year's Eve is always a special occasion for our guests," he says. "We want the food to be as memorable as the festivities themselves." Ice carvings of winter scenes will punctuate the buffet that will feature more than 50 different entrées and side dishes. Dessert service will include the guests' choice of New York cheesecake, bananas Foster, or cherries jubilee.

Joe's Restaurant is open Sunday through Thursday from 6:00 AM to 10:00 PM. Friday and Saturday hours are from 6:00 AM to midnight. Catering facilities are available for groups from 10 to 250.

7

Human Resources

Promotional products are outstanding resources that can motivate personnel, instill commitment to learning in your workforce, build morale and achieve the results you desire from your employees. Through the effective use of proven strategies, you can create a positive atmosphere that fosters team spirit and personal development resulting in amplified production and healthier profits. The benefits of a motivated, focused, and flourishing workforce cannot be emphasized enough.

To understand the power of promotional products in motivation, it's essential to understand the psychology of human motivation. The field of human resources is extremely complex and instilling motivation in the workforce is one of the most important and challenging tasks. Many managers complain that their staffs lack motivation. "If they were only motivated, we could accomplish so much more!" We've got great news for human resources professionals: Every person is motivated. And you are about to learn how to tap into that motivation and harness it to turn your workforce into an inspired team of professionals.

If your staff seems unmotivated, begin by taking a hard look at what you might be doing to discourage them and, equally important, what you are *not* doing to motivate them.

Psychology of Motivation

> We are not in a position in which we have nothing to work with.
> We already have capacities, talents, direction, missions, callings.
>
> —Abraham Maslow

Abraham Maslow was one of the founders of humanistic psychology and probably the greatest contributor to the study and understanding of human motivation. Maslow is well known for his theory of motivation referred to as the "Hierarchy of Needs." His theory indicates that there are five levels of needs that motivate people. Once one level of needs is satisfied, a person's motivation is targeted toward satisfying those needs in the next level. The first level contains the very basic biological and physiological needs including air, water, food, and shelter. The second level includes safety needs like security, stability, and order. The third level is the need for love and belonging; a desire to fit in as a member of a work group; the need for family, affection, and personal relationships. After these low-level needs are fulfilled, people move into the pursuit of esteem, which is the fourth level of Maslow's hierarchy. This level includes self-esteem, achievement, independence, mastery, and status. The fifth level is the highest level that Maslow defined based on a study of the characteristics of highly successful people. Maslow thought this level contained self-actualization needs that are the driving force to realizing one's full personal potential. It is a desire for self-fulfillment, personal growth, and peak experiences.

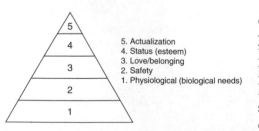

5. Actualization
4. Status (esteem)
3. Love/belonging
2. Safety
1. Physiological (biological needs)

Take a look around your organization and determine how your employees fall into different levels of the hierarchy. You may have employees who are timid and lack self-confidence. Some may be struggling to improve their self-esteem and others who are just bursting with confidence and are driven to be the best that they can be. Wouldn't it be a great accomplishment if as an employer you could propel an employee from the stage of lacking self-confidence to self-actualization? Providing recognition and rewards in the form of promotional products are motivators that can do just that.

Basically, there are two types of motivation: *intrinsic* and *extrinsic*. Intrinsic motivation comes from within while extrinsic motivation is encouragement from an outside source that kicks the intrinsic motivation into gear. Intrinsic motivation is driven by the needs defined in Maslow's hierarchy. For example, if a person is deprived of water, they are in the lowest level of the hierarchy (physiological needs). Their intrinsic motivation will drive them to find water. If an outside source is willing to give them water after they accomplish a specific task, they will be driven to accomplish the task in order to get the reward that fulfills their need. That is somewhat of an archaic example, but it applies throughout the hierarchy. If an individual has low self-esteem, their intrinsic motivation drives them to do things to improve their sense of self-worth. Recognition is an extrinsic motivator that can fulfill the need. By providing that recognition, an employer can improve the employee's job performance and productivity. If an employee is in the stage of motivation that they are striving to realize their full potential, a competition with a promotional product award can feed that desire resulting in greater productivity. It is a win-win situation.

Training

Training and orientation is an essential component to building a thriving business. As important as it is, some employees just don't buy into the process. This leads some business owners and managers to think that training is a waste of time when results are negligible. The truth of the matter is, without formal training, your workforce is grasping at straws to accomplish their daily activities. Therefore, the challenge for human resource professionals is to motivate employees to learn so they can absorb the training, put it to use, experience personal growth, improve their performance, and maximize your business potential.

Effective employee training can:

- Build better communication skills
- Uncover and develop hidden talent
- Ensure quality
- Provide focus
- Enhance commitment
- Decrease turnover
- Grant empowerment

- Multiply productivity
- Reduce absences
- Clarify objectives
- Instill team spirit
- Boost morale
- Escalate sales

So, what is training worth to your business? Do you want a workforce that is there to collect a paycheck or do you want a workforce that is committed to your goals and to taking your business to new horizons? In the next section, we'll explore valuable techniques that arm you with the knowledge to take your workforce to new heights through the use of promotional products.

Is your business full of bickering employees? *"He's not doing his share." "She was late again." "Why do I always get the jobs nobody wants to do?"* Are the employees the problem or is morale the problem? What made your valuable employees so disgruntled? Surely you didn't hire applicants that had a negative outlook. They were probably fresh, excited, and eager to start their new job. However, something has crushed their spirit and turned it into a confrontational, whiny, chip-on-the-shoulder attitude. The first thing you need to do is to review your operation and make sure that everyone is receiving equal and fair treatment. If they are, they just need some morale boosters. If you and your employees are busy settling disputes and stomping out fires, you can't concentrate on business objectives and fulfill your mission. Using promotional products enables you to implement a few simple morale boosters to get your workforce inspired and focused on the big picture.

Training Program

As with any effort, the first thing you want to do is set your goals. What do you wish to accomplish through your employee training and orientation? Do you want your employees to be more intuitive to customer service? Do you want them to learn to cross-sell? Is knowledge of your products or services important? How about reduced clerical errors? Once you know your objectives, you can devise your training session. Develop questions to ask throughout the training to make sure your employees are paying attention and putting information into practice.

Before the training session, fill a basket with wrapped promotional products. Be sure to include gag gifts, higher-value gifts, and useful items in the basket. Get something you can throw at your employees without knocking them down such as a beach ball. The purpose of the ball is to randomly select people to answer questions during training.

> Get their attention, but don't knock them out!

When you finish a section, throw the ball into the air. Whoever catches it answers a question about the section of training you have just completed. After they answer the question, they throw the ball in the air for the next lucky participant to catch. When they answer the question correctly, participants are invited to select a "mystery" gift from the gift basket. Add excitement by allowing employees to "steal" a gift from someone else or select an unwrapped gift from the basket. This reward process accomplishes two things. First, it breaks the monotony of a boring training session and makes it fun. Second, it encourages employees to pay attention so they will be able to answer questions, which equals enhanced learning.

> Fill your basket with goodies to encourage participation.

Motivation and Morale

Next to physical survival, the greatest need of a human being is psychological survival—to be understood, to be affirmed, to be validated, to be appreciated.
—Stephen R. Covey[1]

If you are aiming at increasing the motivation of your staff and improving the morale of your team, it is essential to provide the understanding, affirmation, validation, and appreciation that employees crave. Recognition is a key factor in this motivation and morale building venture. Be sure to recognize:

- Accomplishments
- Desirable behavior

---

[1] Stephen R. Covey, *The 7 Habits of Highly Effective People* (New York: Free Press, 1989).

- Fulfillment of goals
- Extra effort
- Innovation
- Leadership

If you are struggling with poor attendance or tardiness, providing recognition to those who don't exhibit the negative characteristics can ignite desire in others in addition to boosting the morale of the employee who always does everything right. The employees who do what they are supposed to do lose momentum and get discouraged when others around them do not carry their load. Doing the right thing day after day without recognition and putting up with underachievers can wear down even the most high-achieving employees, eroding their motivation and causing them to exhibit the same behaviors that frustrate them. Rather than calling a meeting and remonstrating your employees for excessive absenteeism, present a surprise award recognizing the desired behavior at a regular staff meeting. *"I would like to present a special award to Lisa who has had perfect attendance for the past year. We acknowledge your dedication, Lisa, and truly appreciate it!"*

Recognize desired behavior.

Once you hold a training session, immediately put the newly learned skills into action to enforce them becoming habits. For example, if you are a restaurant owner, you may hold a training session on cross-selling and up-selling, teaching your waitstaff to promote specials, sell before-dinner drinks, desserts, or after-dinner drinks, or to up-sell to a premium wine. Participants learn that increasing ticket amounts can increase tips. By holding a sales competition, you can enhance the knowledge and skills they have gained. If your goal is to increase the sales of a new menu item such as a candy-bar cheesecake, hold a competition and award first-, second- and third-place promotional product prizes to the top-sellers. If you are striving to increase ticket totals, sponsor an "average ticket amount" competition.

Contests and prizes reinforce your training efforts and boost your sales.

If morale problems exist because of a lack of teamwork, promotional products can help build team spirit. Often morale problems exist because of a conflict between shifts. Staff may simply not know each other because of opposing schedules. If this is the case, put opposing parties on the same team with a mission to accomplish a common goal for which they will be rewarded with a promotional product. Choose a goal and set up a competition. Divide staff into teams, taking care to place general opponents on the same team so they will have to work together to win the competition. In team competitions, it is a good idea to award all teams something. Award the most desirable prize for first place, another for second, and another for third. Here are some award occasions to consider:

- Birthdays
- Anniversaries (employment)
- New employees
- Retirement
- Goal attainment
- Academic achievement
- Graduation
- Promotions
- Special personal events

Use promotional products to build team spirit.

Tap into the Power

By now you should fully understand the awesome power of promotional products to increase sales, enhance corporate image, improve employee morale, and so much more. Put them to work for you and enjoy the numerous benefits that can transform your business from a so-so organization to a flourishing, money-making venture with outstanding staff and unwavering community support.

The following is a recap of advantageous programs that will boost your profits, improve your staff, and wow your community.

Advertising
- Sequential direct mail and e-mail
- First-time buyer programs
- Industry news
- Holiday promotions
- Special offers
- Introduction of new products and/or services
- Media advertising with promotional product incentives
- Web advertising with promotional product incentives

Trade Show Marketing
- Professional booths
- Drawings

- Giveaways
- Event sponsorship
- Demonstrations
- Game hosting
- Novelty gifts
- Preshow mailings of partial sets
- Follow-up

Sales Promotions
- Volume order incentives
- Inventory depletion incentives
- Repurchase incentives
- First time buyer programs
- Referral programs
- New product and/or service introductions

Public Relations
- Community involvement
- Event sponsorship
- National charity events
- Health causes
- Welfare causes
- Political efforts
- Education
- Athletics
- Fund raising
- Youth development
- Safety training
- Character development

Human Resources
- Training and orientation
- Motivation
- Morale improvement

- Team building
- Recognition
- Acknowledgment
- Awards
- Rewards
- Competitions

Promotional products deliver lasting value and impact that conventional advertising just can't provide. Long after an advertising message disappears, promotional items imprinted with your logo or message offer a tangible reminder of your company—and they are far more cost-effective and accessible than conventional advertising. Whether you're a Fortune 100 company, a small business, or a nonprofit organization, imprinted promotional products offer a promotional solution that's appropriate for you. Put promotional products to work for you today and take your business to the next level!

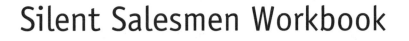

Silent Salesmen Workbook

The following section is an excerpt from the *Xtreme Business Workbook*, available at www.thesilentsalesmen.com:

Critical Causes of Business Failure

1. Under funding
2. Lack of operating capital
3. Poor business management practices
4. Poor location
5. Lack of entrepreneurial skills and foresight

The Most Common Causes of Business Failure

- Lack of effective Acquisition and Retention systems.
- Most businesses fail because they don't have enough customers buying from them regularly and profitably. (Acquisition)
- They're not utilizing the skills necessary to keep their customers from defecting to the competition. (Retention)
- Getting and keeping profitable customers must be a businesses number one priority.

Your Most Important Business Asset

- Your Customers and Clients

Your Most Important Business Skill and Number One Priority
- Knowing how to cost-effectively attract and keep an adequate number of loyal and profitable customers.

The New Reality

It is no longer possible for a business to maintain a competitive advantage for an extended period of time because of the products or services they offer, or the prices they charge.

If you keep on doing what you've always done,
You'll never get better over the long run.
If you keep on thinking what you've always thought,
You'll keep on getting what life's always brought.
If you keep on being who you've always been,
You'll keep on taking it on the chin.

Two laws to work by are:

1. Law of Averages
   - Work harder.
   - Focus on quantity.
2. Law of Efficiency
   - Work strategically.
   - Focus on quality.

To achieve something you've never done before, you're going to have to become someone you've never been before. To make minor changes in your behavior and results, change your attitude. To make quantum leaps in your behavior and results, change your thinking.

You're not in the (furniture, restaurant, plumbing, mortgage, insurance, etc.) business . . . you're in the business of running a business that happens to sell those products and services and other related products and services to people for a profit.

> The significant problems we face today cannot be solved at the same level of thinking as when we created them.
> —Albert Einstein

Three Critical Questions
1. How would a marketer think?
2. What would make people want to listen to me?
3. How can I get people to listen, and compel them to take action?

It's as useless to try to sell a man something until you have first made him want to listen, as it would be to command the earth to stop rotating.

—Napoleon Hill

Business Profile

Assign one of the following numbers to each component to reevaluate your present business: Thrilled = 5, Happy = 4, Okay = 3, Bummer = 2, Worried = 1.

Component	Present Number	Satisfaction Level	Number in 3 years	Areas of Immediate Change
Size of your business				
Number of customers or clients				
Segmentation of customer database				
Number of past customers				
Segmentation of database				
Number of prospects				
Segmentation of database				
Number of staff				
Quality of staff				
Effectiveness of staff				

(*Continued*)

Component	Present Number	Satisfaction Level	Number in 3 years	Areas of Immediate Change
Number of customers per employee				
Gross dollars per employee				
Office/store location				
Expense ratio				
Effectiveness of advertising				
Relationship with customers				
Relationship with vendors				
Gross income				
Net income				
Number of hours worked				
Free personal time				
Quality/amount of follow up service				
Monthly production				

Focus on the Future

Describe what you would like your business to look like three years from now:

_____

_____

_____

_____

_____

_____

      Imagine you're one of your customers three years from now. Describe your experience in doing business with you or your business (in your customer's words):

_____

_____

_____

_____

_____

_____

What has to happen between now and then, for your business to actually look like you described?

_____

_____

_____

_____

_____

Things in your control:

_____

_____

_____

_____

_____

Things not in your control:

_____

_____

_____

_____

_____

What back-up plans do you need to put in place to compensate for the things you have no (or limited) control over?

_____

_____

_____

_____

_____

Who are the people/what are the resources you need to help you accomplish your three-year goal?

_____

_____

_____

_____

_____

What Business Are You In?

My prospects contact me (or my business) for the products and/or services we offer because:

_____

_____

_____

_____

_____

My customers or clients make repeat purchases with me or my business because:

_____

_____

_____

_____

_____

What Are Your Primary Methods of Attracting New Business?

Source of New Business	Number of New Clients per Month from This Source	Percent of Total New Clients from This Source
1.		%
2.		%
3.		%

4.		%
5.		%

My most effective customer acquisition system is:

_____

_____

_____

_____

The reason it's so effective (or that I like or use it so much) is:

_____

_____

_____

_____

The most under-utilized system with the greatest potential is:

_____

_____

_____

_____

The reason I don't use it more often is:

_____

_____

_____

_____

What can I do to make it more useable or more effective in my business?

_____

_____

_____
_____
_____
_____

Breaking the Preoccupation Barrier

1. Why are you bothering me?
2. So what? Who cares?
3. Why should I believe you? (WIIFM?)
4. Why should I do something about this now?

Effective Marketing Is Making People _Want_ to Listen to You

- Speak their language.
- Think like they think.
- Feel like they feel.
- See what they see.
- Live like they live.
- Experience what they experience.
- _Become one of them._

Seven Emotional Appeals That Stimulate Action

To create a successful business you have to sell something.

In order to sell something, your prospects have to listen to your sales story.

In order for them to listen to your sales story, it has to be appealing to them so they'll _want_ to listen.

Seven Emotional Appeals

1. Greed
2. Exclusivity
3. Salvation
4. Fear
5. Guilt

6. Anger

7. Flattery

Action Plan

A well-known philosopher once said, "Ideas are like slippery fish. Unless you capture them with the point of a pen or pencil, they'll slip away never to be seen again." But, merely capturing is not enough. Unless you actually do something with either the fish or the idea, neither will be of much value to you.

Use this page to record the best ideas you got from this section, how you plan to implement them your business, and who you'll share the ideas with. Reliable studies clearly demonstrate that if you teach or share with someone an idea you've learned, your personal understanding and retention of that idea are dramatically enhanced.

Idea 1:

_____

_____

_____

_____

_____

_____

How I plan to use it in my business:

_____

_____

_____

_____

_____

Who I'll share this idea with:

_____

_____

Idea 2:

_____

_____

_____
_____
_____
_____

How I plan to use it in my business:

_____
_____
_____
_____
_____

Who I'll share this idea with:

_____
_____

Idea 3:

_____
_____
_____
_____
_____

How I plan to use it in my business:

_____
_____
_____
_____
_____

Who I'll share this idea with:

_____
_____

Identify Your Target Market

All prospects are not of equal value. For example:

Great Clients
- Busy
- Do what they enjoy
- Coachable
- Responsible
- Time is precious
- Not pushovers or laydowns
- Like business relationships
- Receptive

Sometimes Worth-Helping Clients
- Not yet great clients, but have potential
- Sound like great clients, but are weak in follow-through
- Need more hand-holding
- Hesitate to make commitments
- Have good intentions, but struggle to stay on track
- Need someone to encourage them to do what they know will be wise
- A relationship with them may or may not be profitable
- You must be firm
- Do not tolerate any deviation from commitments
- Don't waste too much time with them
- They need your strength and discipline more than anything else you can give them

Fun but Hopeless Clients
- Genuinely nice people, but lousy clients
- Appear sincere and motivated, but never follow through
- Smart enough to know what to do, but lack the discipline to change their "fatal" habits
- Sometimes burdened with so much debt that they're embarrassed to tell you the truth

- Rarely get the information you need to you
- Think that having a good excuse for not taking action is as good as taking action
- Have a lifestyle that is much bigger than their financial reality
- Tend to be unrealistically optimistic

Uses-You-for-Information Clients

- Have the discipline to make decisions, and enjoys doing research
- Use you for information, then buy from cheapest source
- Believe this is perfectly legitimate
- Have low opinions of agents, and have no qualms about taking advantage of them
- Often refuse to answer questions, say: "Just tell me what you have!"
- Want solutions from you, saying: "Here's my situation. What would you do?"
- Often clever enough to make you question whether your approach is reasonable
- Tend to play devil's advocate, taking either side in any issue
- Seem to derive their self-worth from getting something for nothing
- More interested in showing you how smart they are than in seeking your help
- The best you can do for yourself is to identify these users quickly and run

Doesn't-Trust-Anybody Client

- Expect to be betrayed in their minds
- Danger lurks around the next corner
- Treat you suspiciously from the start (You're guilty until proven innocent.)
- Suspicious when you ask the questions you need to ask in order to help them
- Have stories about how their business relationships always sour
- Just "know" there is an angle there somewhere, and they only need a little time to find it

The best you can do for yourself is to recognize these nontrusters quickly, feel a little sorry for them, and leave them to their paranoia

Identify Your Target Market Worksheet 1

Product or Service:

_____

_____

Describe the demographics and psychographics of your current book of business or customer base (Demographics = Who buys; psychographics = why they buy):

_____

_____

_____

_____

_____

_____

Describe your ideal or model customer:

_____

_____

_____

_____

_____

_____

Describe the type of customer you would like to do more business with:

_____

_____

_____

_____

_____

_____

How is this market accessible?

_____

_____

_____
_____
_____
_____

How sophisticated are they (what do they already know about the type of products or services you sell)?

_____
_____
_____
_____
_____

What should they, or what would they like to know?

_____
_____
_____
_____
_____

Do you possess the knowledge, skill, and ability to provide them with this information?

☐   Yes

☐   No

If not, what would it take for you to acquire those abilities?

_____
_____
_____
_____
_____

Identify Your Target Market Worksheet 2

Product or service:

_____
_____

Describe the demographics and psychographics of your current book of business or customer base (demographics = Who buys; psychographics = why they buy):

_____

_____

_____

_____

_____

_____

Describe your ideal or model customer:

_____

_____

_____

_____

_____

_____

Describe the type of customer you would like to do more business with:

_____

_____

_____

_____

_____

_____

How is this market accessible?

_____

_____

_____

_____

_____

How sophisticated are they (what do they already know about the type of products or services you sell)?

_____

_____

_____

_____

_____

_____

What should they, or what would they like to know?

_____

_____

_____

_____

_____

_____

Do you posses the knowledge, skill and ability to provide them with this information?

☐   Yes

☐   No

If not, what would it take for you to acquire those abilities?

_____

_____

_____

_____

_____

_____

Identify Your Target Market Worksheet 3

Product or service:

_____

_____

Describe the demographics and psychographics of your current book of business or customer base (demographics = Who buys; psychographics = why they buy):

_____

_____

_____

_____

_____

_____

Describe your ideal or model customer:

_____

_____

_____

_____

_____

Describe the type of customer you would like to do more business with:

_____

_____

_____

_____

_____

How is this market accessible?

_____

_____

_____

_____

_____

How sophisticated are they (what do they already know about the type of products or services you sell)?

_____

_____

_____

_____

What should they, or what would they like to know?

_____

_____

_____

_____
_____
_____

Do you posses the knowledge, skill and ability to provide them with this information?

☐　Yes
☐　No

If not, what would it take for you to acquire those abilities?

_____
_____
_____
_____
_____
_____

Identify Your Target Market Worksheet 4

Product or Service:

_____
_____

Describe the demographics and psychographics of your current book of business or customer base (demographics = Who buys; psychographics = why they buy):

_____
_____
_____
_____
_____
_____

Describe your ideal or model customer:

_____
_____
_____
_____
_____
_____

Describe the type of customer you would like to do more business with:

_____

_____

_____

_____

_____

_____

How is this market accessible?

_____

_____

_____

_____

_____

How sophisticated are they (what do they already know about the type of products or services you sell)?

_____

_____

_____

_____

_____

What should they, or what would they like to know?

_____

_____

_____

_____

_____

Do you posses the knowledge, skill and ability to provide them with this information?

☐ Yes

☐ No

If not, what would it take for you to acquire those abilities?

_____

_____

_____

_____

_____

_____

Examples of Target Markets (Insurance)

Auto Insurance

- Driving record
- Type of vehicle
- Use of vehicle
- Age of driver(s)
- Occupation of owner
- Claims history of owner
- Credit report status

Homeowners Insurance

- Value of property
- Location of property
- Age of structure
- Use of property
- Value of personal property
- Claims history of property
- Claims history of owner
- Credit report status

Life/Health/Disability Insurance

- Age of prospect
- Occupation of prospect
- Health of prospect
- Family of prospect
- Value of assets of prospect
- Dreams, goals, aspirations of prospect

Commercial Insurance

- Type of property/business
- Use of property
- Value of property
- Age of structures
- Size of business
- Number of employees
- Gross income

Target Markets by Event or Affinity

- Newly purchased home
- Weddings
- Divorce
- Death
- Births
- Family addition
- Graduation
- Retirement
- Job promotion
- Job transfer
- Newly purchased vehicle
- Newly acquired possessions
- Inheritance
- Start up of a business
- Closing of a business
- Hiring new employees
- Laying off employees
- Plant or business expansion
- Plant or business consolidation
- Plant or business sale
- Plant or business acquisition
- Announcement of new products/service
- Acquisition of new equipment

- Occupation
- Club membership
- Professional association
- Alumni associations
- Church affiliation
- Neighborhood association
- Children's teams/events
- Joint venture arrangements
- Purchased lists
- Compiled lists

Identify Your Target Market's Wants

What *end result* do your prospective customers want from:

1. Your product or service
2. Doing business with you

Determine Who You Will Survey

- Suspects
- Prospects
- Shoppers
- Customers
- Clients
- Advocates
- Raving fans
- Former clients

Design a Needs and Wants Analysis Questionnaire

- What do they expect from this type of product or service?
- How long have they used this type of product or service?
- What has been their experience in the past?
- What is their biggest frustration with the products/services they've used in the past?

- What do they expect from the provider (company) of this service?

- What is their past history/experience with other salespeople?

- What is their biggest frustration with businesses in this field or area?

- What made them choose the type of product or service they currently have?

- What made them choose the particular salesperson or company they're currently with?

- What is the most important consideration for choosing this type of product/service?

- What is the most important consideration for choosing a sales person or company?

- If they had a magic wand and could construct an ideal buying experience, what would it look like?

- If they could construct an ideal ongoing client/salesperson/ company relationship, what would it look like?

- How often would they like to be contacted with new information, or be contacted by their salesperson or company service person?

- Do they prefer being contacted by phone, mail, or e-mail?

- Do they prefer being contacted at home or at work?

Customer Questionnaire Template

Your opinions about our products and services are extremely important to us. We use them to help us make sure that we are providing the best service possible at all times.

If you'll take just a minute to answer a couple of questions and send this back to us, we'll send you a certificate for a *free* dinner for two at one of our fine local restaurants.

Name: _____

Phone: _____

Address: _____

City: _____ State: _____ Zip: _____

E-mail: _____

Which product or service did you buy?

_____

1. Have you ever purchased the same or similar product or service from another company?

   ☐ Yes
   ☐ No

2. Name of company: _____

3. Why did you decide to purchase from us?

   _____
   _____
   _____
   _____
   _____
   _____

4. Are you happy with the product or service you purchased?

   ☐ Yes
   ☐ No

5. Were you pleased with the treatment you received from us?

   ☐ Yes
   ☐ No

6. What suggestions do you have that would make it easier to do business with us?

   _____
   _____
   _____
   _____
   _____
   _____

7. What suggestions do you have that would make our products or services provide more benefit or value to you?

   _____
   _____
   _____
   _____
   _____
   _____

8. Please write a one-sentence summary of how the product or service you purchased from us, or how doing business with us has benefited you: ·

9. Would you be willing to refer others to us who might consider purchasing the products or services we offer?

    ☐   Yes

    ☐   No

10. May we share your comments with others who may be considering doing business with us?

    ☐   Yes

    ☐   No

Prioritize Your Target Market's Wants	Priority
What do your Prospects/Customers want most from the Products and Services you sell?	

(*Continued*)

What do your Prospects/Customers want most from the salesperson or company they do business with?	Priority

Prospect's/Customer's Overall Top Five Wants
1.
2.
3.
4.
5.

Action Plan

A well-known philosopher once said, "Ideas are like slippery fish. Unless you capture them with the point of a pen or pencil, they'll slip away never to be seen again." But merely capturing is not enough. Unless you actually do something with either the fish or the idea, neither will be of much value to you.

Use this page to record the best ideas you got from this section, how you plan to implement them in your business, and who you'll share the ideas with. Reliable studies clearly demonstrate that if you teach or share with someone an idea you've learned, your personal understanding and retention of that idea are dramatically enhanced.

Idea 1:

_____
_____
_____
_____
_____
_____

How I plan to use it in my business:

_____
_____
_____
_____
_____

Who I'll share this idea with:

_____
_____

Idea 2:

_____
_____
_____
_____
_____
_____

How I plan to use it in my business:

_____
_____
_____
_____

_____
_____

Who I'll share this idea with:

_____
_____

Idea 3:

_____
_____
_____
_____
_____
_____

How I plan to use it in my business:

_____
_____
_____
_____
_____
_____

Who I'll share this idea with:

_____
_____

Identify and Analyze Your Competition

Competitive Questionnaire 1

Name of competitor:_____
    Company: _____
    Location: _____
    Phone: _____
    Web Site:_____
    Person talked to:_____

How long have they been in business?

_____

How many employees do they have?

_____

What are their hours of operation?

_____

What particular strengths do they possess?

_____
_____
_____
_____
_____

What uniqueness do they possess?

_____
_____
_____
_____
_____

What can they offer the market that you can't?

_____
_____
_____
_____
_____

What weakness do they have that you can exploit?

_____
_____
_____
_____
_____

Did they attempt to do a wants analysis on me?

_____

Did they attempt to get me to come to their place of business?

_____

Is theirs largely a phone-based, quote-providing service?

_____

Did they ask about other products or services that I might need, or that might enable me to get a discount?

_____

Did they attempt to determine my level of understanding of the products or services I was inquiring about, then help educate or inform me with regard to my particular needs?

_____
_____
_____
_____
_____

Did they attempt to explain the differences and benefits of doing business with them?

_____
_____
_____
_____
_____

Did they get my name, address, and phone number, and tell me they'd send me some follow up information?

_____

Did I get the feeling they really cared about me as a person, and not "just another sale or commission?"

_____

If I were a "real" prospect, would I want to drop the phone and rush to their place of business because of either the feeling I had in my conversation with them, or the information they provided me, made me feel that they really had my best interests in mind, and that this is the best option I have to choose from?

Competitive Questionnaire 2

Name of competitor:_____
     Company: _____
     Location: _____
     Phone: _____
     Web Site:_____
     Person talked to:_____
     How long have they been in business?

     How many employees do they have?

     What are their hours of operation?

     What particular strengths do they possess?

     What uniqueness do they possess?

     What can they offer the market that you can't?

What weakness do they have that you can exploit?

_____
_____
_____
_____
_____
_____

Did they attempt to do a wants analysis on me?

_____

Did they attempt to get me to come to their place of business?

_____

Is theirs largely a phone-based, quote-providing service?

_____

Did they ask about other products or services that I might need, or that might enable me to get a discount?

_____

Did they attempt to determine my level of understanding of the products or services I was inquiring about, then help educate or inform me with regard to my particular needs?

_____
_____
_____
_____
_____
_____

Did they attempt to explain the differences and benefits of doing business with them?

_____
_____
_____
_____
_____
_____

Did they get my name, address, and phone number, and tell me they'd send me some follow up information?

_____

Did I get the feeling they really cared about me as a person, and not "just another sale or commission?"

_____

If I were a "real" prospect, would I want to drop the phone and rush to their place of business because of either the feeling I had in my conversation with them, or the information they provided me, made me feel that they really had my best interests in mind, and that this is the best option I have to choose from?

Competitive Questionnaire 3

Name of competitor:_____

    Company: _____

    Location: _____

    Phone: _____

    Web Site:_____

    Person talked to:_____

    How long have they been in business?

_____

    How many employees do they have?

_____

    What are their hours of operation?

_____

    What particular strengths do they possess?

_____
_____
_____
_____
_____

    What uniqueness do they possess?

_____
_____
_____
_____
_____

What can they offer the market that you can't?

_____
_____
_____
_____
_____
_____

What weakness do they have that you can exploit?

_____
_____
_____
_____
_____
_____

Did they attempt to do a wants analysis on me?

_____

Did they attempt to get me to come to their place of business?

_____

Is theirs largely a phone-based, quote-providing service?

_____

Did they ask about other products or services that I might need, or that might enable me to get a discount?

_____

Did they attempt to determine my level of understanding of the products or services I was inquiring about, then help educate or inform me with regard to my particular needs?

_____
_____
_____
_____

Did they attempt to explain the differences and benefits of doing business with them?

_____

_____

_____

_____

_____

_____

Did they get my name, address, and phone number, and tell me they'd send me some follow up information?

_____

Did I get the feeling they really cared about me as a person, and not "just another sale or commission?"

_____

If I were a "real" prospect, would I want to drop the phone and rush to their place of business because of either the feeling I had in my conversation with them, or the information they provided me, made me feel that they really had my best interests in mind, and that this is the best option I have to choose from?

Competitive Questionnaire 4

Name of competitor:_____

    Company: _____

    Location: _____

    Phone: _____

    Web Site:_____

    Person talked to: _____

    How long have they been in business?

_____

How many employees do they have?

_____

What are their hours of operation?

_____

What particular strengths do they possess?

_____

_____

_____

_____

_____

What uniqueness do they possess?

_____
_____
_____
_____
_____
_____

What can they offer the market that you can't?

_____
_____
_____
_____
_____
_____

What weakness do they have that you can exploit?

_____
_____
_____
_____
_____
_____

Did they attempt to do a wants analysis on me?

_____

Did they attempt to get me to come to their place of business?

_____

Is theirs largely a phone-based, quote-providing service?

_____

Did they ask about other products or services that I might need, or that might enable me to get a discount?

_____

Did they attempt to determine my level of understanding of the products or services I was inquiring about, then help educate or inform me with regard to my particular needs?

_____
_____
_____
_____

_____

_____

Did they attempt to explain the differences and benefits of doing business with them?

_____

_____

_____

_____

_____

_____

Did they get my name, address, and phone number, and tell me they'd send me some follow up information?

_____

Did I get the feeling they really cared about me as a person, and not "just another sale or commission?"

_____

If I were a "real" prospect, would I want to drop the phone and rush to their place of business because of either the feeling I had in my conversation with them, or the information they provided me, made me feel that they really had my best interests in mind, and that this is the best option I have to choose from?

Competitive Questionnaire 5

Name of competitor:_____
    Company: _____
    Location: _____
    Phone: _____
    Web Site:_____
    Person talked to:_____
    How long have they been in business?

_____

How many employees do they have?

_____

What are their hours of operation?

_____

What particular strengths do they possess?

_____

_____

_____

_____

_____

What uniqueness do they possess?

_____

_____

_____

_____

_____

What can they offer the market that you can't?

_____

_____

_____

_____

_____

What weakness do they have that you can exploit?

_____

_____

_____

_____

_____

Did they attempt to do a wants analysis on me?

_____

Did they attempt to get me to come to their place of business?

_____

Is theirs largely a phone-based, quote-providing service?

_____

Did they ask about other products or services that I might need, or that might enable me to get a discount?

_____

Did they attempt to determine my level of understanding of the products or services I was inquiring about, then help educate or inform me with regard to my particular needs?

_____
_____
_____
_____
_____

Did they attempt to explain the differences and benefits of doing business with them?

_____
_____
_____
_____
_____

Did they get my name, address, and phone number, and tell me they'd send me some follow up information?

_____

Did I get the feeling they really cared about me as a person, and not "just another sale or commission?"

_____

If I were a "real" prospect, would I want to drop the phone and rush to their place of business because of either the feeling I had in my conversation with them, or the information they provided me, made me feel that they really had my best interests in mind, and that this is the best option I have to choose from?

Comparative Analysis 1

Priority:

_____

How my business handles/solves/satisfies this priority:

_____
_____
_____
_____
_____
_____

What (name of competitor) does:

_____
_____
_____
_____
_____

The downside in dealing with them is:

_____
_____
_____
_____

The advantage in dealing with me/us is:

_____
_____
_____
_____
_____

The ideal way to handle this would be to:

_____
_____
_____
_____

What this would mean to the prospect/customer is:

_____
_____

_____

_____

_____

_____

What steps we need to take to achieve that ideal situation:

_____

_____

_____

_____

_____

Comparative Analysis 2

Priority:

_____

How my business handles/solves/satisfies this priority:

_____

_____

_____

_____

_____

What (name of competitor) does:

_____

_____

_____

_____

_____

The downside in dealing with them is:

_____

_____

_____

_____

_____

The advantage in dealing with me/us is:

_____
_____
_____
_____
_____

The ideal way to handle this would be to:

_____
_____
_____
_____
_____

What this would mean to the prospect/customer is:

_____
_____
_____
_____
_____

What steps we need to take to achieve that ideal situation:

_____
_____
_____
_____
_____

Comparative Analysis 3

Priority:

_____

How my business handles/solves/satisfies this priority:

_____
_____
_____
_____

What (name of competitor) does:

The downside in dealing with them is:

The advantage in dealing with me/us is:

The ideal way to handle this would be to:

What this would mean to the prospect/customer is:

What steps we need to take to achieve that ideal situation:

_____
_____
_____
_____
_____
_____

Comparative Analysis 4

Priority:

_____

How my business handles/solves/satisfies this priority:

_____
_____
_____
_____
_____
_____

What (name of competitor) does:

_____
_____
_____
_____
_____
_____

The downside in dealing with them is:

_____
_____
_____
_____
_____
_____

The advantage in dealing with me/us is:

_____
_____
_____

_____

_____

_____

The ideal way to handle this would be to:

_____

_____

_____

_____

_____

What this would mean to the prospect/customer is:

_____

_____

_____

_____

_____

What steps we need to take to achieve that ideal situation:

_____

_____

_____

_____

_____

Comparative Analysis 5

Priority:

_____

How my business handles/solves/satisfies this priority:

_____

_____

_____

_____

_____

What (name of competitor) does:

_____

_____

_____

_____

_____

The downside in dealing with them is:

_____

_____

_____

_____

_____

The advantage in dealing with me/us is:

_____

_____

_____

_____

_____

The ideal way to handle this would be to:

_____

_____

_____

_____

_____

What this would mean to the prospect/customer is:

_____

_____

_____

_____

_____

What steps we need to take to achieve that ideal situation:

_____

_____
_____
_____
_____
_____

Action Plan

A well-known philosopher once said, "Ideas are like slippery fish. Unless you capture them with the point of a pen or pencil, they'll slip away never to be seen again." But merely capturing is not enough. Unless you actually do something with either the fish or the idea, neither will be of much value to you.

Use this page to record the best ideas you got from this section, how you plan to implement them in your business, and who you'll share the ideas with. Reliable studies clearly demonstrate that if you teach or share with someone an idea you've learned, your personal understanding and retention of that idea are dramatically enhanced.

Idea 1:

_____
_____
_____
_____
_____

How I plan to use it in my business:

_____
_____
_____
_____
_____

Who I'll share this idea with:

_____
_____

Idea 2:

_____

_____

_____

_____

_____

_____

How I plan to use it in my business:

_____

_____

_____

_____

_____

Who I'll share this idea with:

_____

_____

Idea 3:

_____

_____

_____

_____

_____

_____

How I plan to use it in my business:

_____

_____

_____

_____

_____

Who I'll share this idea with:

_____

_____

Entice Your Prospects to Contact You

Thirteen critical questions all prospects must answer before they buy, or that all customers must answer before they purchase from you again include:

1. Do I want the benefits this product or service provides?
2. Is this the right product or service?
3. Is this the right manufacturer or producing company to buy from?
4. Is this the right store, shop, or business to buy from?
5. Are you the right salesperson to buy from?
6. Is this the right price to pay for this product or service?
7. Is this the right time to buy (invest)?
8. How do I pay for it?
9. What if it's not right for me, I don't like it, don't want it, or change my mind?
10. IIow can I be assured that I'm getting the best value for the money I'm about to spend?
11. Why should I do business with you, instead of any and all other options I have—including doing nothing at all?
12. What are the most common mistakes other people make when buying this type of product or service?
13. How can I avoid making those same mistakes?

Identifying Your Unique Comparative Advantage

To find your unique comparative advantage, you will need to lay some groundwork. This section will help you do that.

Important Terms
- UCA Unique Competitive Advantage
- UCA Unique Comparative Advantage
- USP Unique Selling Proposition
- UPA Unique Purchase Appeal
- SOB Statement of Benefit

- USA Unique Selling Advantage
- PDF Personal Differentiating Factor
- UDF—Unique Differentiating Factor

Find an Unfilled Need or Problem in Your Market or Industry

- Lack of choice, selections, styles, services, products, or options
- Quality of products and/or services
- Advice, education, or assistance
- Guarantee or warranty
- Price competitiveness
- Location, delivery, convenience
- Incentives, premiums, bonuses
- Trade-ins, upgrades, add-ons, or "bundles"

Where to Get Your Information

- Observe your market
- Ask your customers
- Get on your competitor's mailing lists
- Buy competitor's products
- Ask your employees
- Ask your suppliers or vendors
- Observe other related and nonrelated markets and businesses

Make a Selection Based on:

- Why your prospects contact your business for the products and/ or services you offer
- Why they actually buy from you the first time
- Why your customers or clients make repeat purchases from your business
- The greatest market need or problem
- Your superior ability to solve a need or problem
- The greatest potential or opportunity

Competitive Analysis

- What is your competition doing to address this need or problem?
- Direct competition
- Indirect competition
- Inertia

Determine Your Ability and Feasibility to Satisfy or Solve the Problem

- Physical resources
- Time resources
- Financial resources
- Employee resources
- Potential for profit . . . long term/short term
- Potential for leverage
- Calculate the downsides

Advantages of Doing Business with Me (or My Business) Are

- Exclusive niche
- Expertise
- Guarantee
- Market positioning
- Price
- Payment
- Product selection
- Freebies or premiums
- Advice and assistance
- Convenience
- Hidden benefit
- Consumer education
- Celebrity endorsement
- Presentation style
- Affinity
- Quality of products/services
- Other

Prioritize and List

Benefits or Advantages of Doing Business with You	Benefits Exclusive to You	You and Your Competition Offer	Both Offer; They Don't Capitalize On
1.			
2.			
3.			
4.			
5.			
6.			
7.			
8.			

Articulate Your Statement

- Be clear, concise, and specific . . . not vague.
- Don't use clichés or platitudes.
- Be compelling.
- Be unique, special . . . different.
- Don't be cute or clever.
- Be bold.
- Be benefit driven.
- Be the "firstest" with the "mostest."
- Appeal to one solution per UCA.

Always think in terms of the customer: What's in it for me?

Formulate Your Statement

A. Formula One

1. You know how (point out a common problem your customers face) . . .

_____
_____
_____
_____
_____
_____

2. Well, what I do is (provide a solution to that problem) . . .

_____
_____
_____
_____
_____

B. Formula Two

I help people (solve a particular problem) . . .

_____
_____
_____
_____
_____

By:

_____
_____
_____
_____
_____

Or,
I'm in the business of (providing a solution to a particular problem) . . .

_____
_____
_____

_____
_____

By:

_____
_____
_____
_____
_____
_____

C. Informative Reply

In response to the question, "Why should I consider doing business with you," complete the following sentence: "My customers tell me . . ."

_____
_____
_____
_____
_____
_____

Effective Marketing

Effective marketing is contacting your target market at the right time, with a message that entices, compels—nearly forces them to contact you to learn more. When you pursue prospects, they perceive you as a salesperson and go on the defensive. When they contact you, they perceive you to be an advisor or consultant, and are open and receptive.

You've identified your target market(s). You know what they want from the products/services you provide, and from a salesperson and company.

You know the strengths/weakness of your competition, and how they satisfy those wants.

You know the advantages of purchasing your products/services, and doing business with you.

You must now find a way to let your prospects know of those advantages, and provide an incentive for them to contact you to learn more.

Timing is critical. When is the ideal time to contact your target market for:

Product or Service 1:

_____

_____

_____

_____

Product or Service 2:

_____

_____

_____

_____

Product or Service 3:

_____

_____

_____

_____

Product or Service 4:

_____

_____

_____

_____

Getting More New Customers

> I don't know the one secret to marketing success, but I do know the biggest reason for marketing failure, which is trying to be all things to all people.
>
> —Joe Stumpf

Primary Methods of Attracting New Business

Source of New Business	Number of New Customers per Month from This Source	Percent of Total New Customers from This Source

(Continued)

Source of New Business	Number of New Customers per Month from This Source	Percent of Total New Customers from This Source

1. Select Your Target Markets

   a. Primary

   b. Secondary

My ideal customer or client is a person, family, or business who:

_____

_____

_____

_____

_____

_____

I would like to have more of these types of clients because:

_____

_____

_____

_____

_____

_____

2. Determine the Best Methods of Reaching Your Prospects

   a. Medium

What media sources can I use to get in front of my prospective clients or customers?

_____

_____

_____

_____
_____
_____

How can I *cost-effectively* reach a *large number* of my potential customers?

_____
_____
_____
_____
_____

How can I best reach *high-potential, highly leverageable* individual prospects?

_____
_____
_____
_____
_____

Methods of Contact (Medium)

- Telemarketing
- Letters
- Postcards
- Flyers
- Door hangers
- Newspaper ads
- Magazine ads
- Trade journal ads/articles
- Industry newsletter ads/articles
- School newsletter ads/articles
- Personal newsletters
- Inserts
- Press releases
- Yellow Pages
- White Pages
- Billboards/posters
- Bus Stop Benches
- Radio ads
- Television ads
- Host a radio program
- Host a TV program
- Business cards
- Supermarket bulletin boards
- Classified ads
- Centers of influence
- Joint ventures
- Referrals

- Purchase/rent database lists
- Piggyback invoice mailings
- Fax blasting
- Val-pak ads
- Taxi signs
- Movie theatres
- Sponsorships
- Internet/web pages
- Building signage
- In-office displays
- Window displays
- Shopping center promotions
- Bumper stickers
- Refrigerator magnets
- Remembrance give-away items
- Client contests/competitions
- Staff contests/competitions
- Strategic alliances
- Author a book
- Write special reports
- Seminars
- Open houses
- Teach classes
- Sponsor scholarships
- On-hold messages
- Point-of-sale displays
- VCR clips
- Audio business cards
- Reprint press articles

An additional method of contact I can use immediately in my business is:

_____

_____

_____

_____

_____

_____

The message I will convey is:

_____

_____

_____

_____

_____

How I plan to use this:

_____

_____

_____

_____

_____

_____

The results I expect to get from using this are:

_____

_____

_____

_____

_____

_____

An additional method of contact I can use immediately in my business is:

_____

_____

_____

_____

_____

The message I will convey is:

_____

_____

_____

_____

_____

How I plan to use this:

_____

_____

_____

_____

_____

The results I expect to get from using this are:

_____

_____

_____
_____
_____
_____

An additional method of contact I can use immediately in my business is:

_____
_____
_____
_____
_____
_____

The message I will convey is:

_____
_____
_____
_____
_____
_____

How I plan to use this:

_____
_____
_____
_____
_____
_____

The results I expect to get from using this are:

_____
_____
_____
_____
_____
_____

An additional method of contact I can use immediately in my business is:

_____

_____

_____

_____

_____

_____

The message I will convey is:

_____

_____

_____

_____

_____

_____

How I plan to use this:

_____

_____

_____

_____

The results I expect to get from using this are:

_____

_____

_____

_____

_____

B. Timing

When are my prospects most receptive, or when are they most likely to need my products and/or services?

_____

_____

_____

_____

_____

C. Message

What types of benefits would my "large number" of prospects be most responsive to?

_____

_____

_____

_____

_____

_____

What types of benefits would my "high-potential, highly lever-ageable" prospects be most responsive to?

_____

_____

_____

_____

_____

_____

Examples include:

- Save money/reduce costs
- Better coverage
- Higher rate of return
- Lower interest rates
- Discounts for multiple purchases
- Multiple services in one location
- One person to deal with
- Develop a personal relationship with staff or employees and know who you're dealing with each time you call
- More convenient location
- Friendly staff
- Abundant educational materials/handouts
- More convenient times

3. Compel Your Prospects to Contact You

A. When you call them, you're perceived as a salesperson.

B. When they call you, you're perceived as a consultant or advisor.

What could I possibly say that would create enough interest and desire in my prospects for them to unhesitatingly, nearly automatically, act on the message I conveyed to them?

_____

_____

_____

_____

_____

_____

4. Educate Them and Motivate, Compel—in Fact, Nearly Force Them to Want to Meet with You

A. Establish yourself as an expert—the only person who can solve their problems, or

B. Establish your business as the only logical and rational choice they have to do business with

What kinds of educational materials can I use to establish myself as an expert, or my business as, not only the logical choice, but the only choice for my prospects to do business with?

Printed Materials:

_____

_____

_____

_____

_____

Audio Cassettes or Videotapes:

_____

_____

_____

_____

_____

Action Plan

A well-known philosopher once said, "Ideas are like slippery fish. Unless you capture them with the point of a pen or pencil, they'll slip away never to be seen again." But, merely capturing is not enough. Unless you actually do something with either the fish or the idea, neither will be of much value to you.

Use this page to record the best ideas you got from this section, how you plan to implement them in your business, and who you'll share the ideas with. Reliable studies clearly demonstrate that if you teach or share with someone an idea you've learned, your personal understanding and retention of that idea are dramatically enhanced.

Idea 1:

_____

_____

_____

_____

_____

_____

How I plan to use it in my business:

_____

_____

_____

_____

_____

_____

Who I'll share this idea with:

_____

_____

Idea 2:

_____

_____

_____

_____

_____

_____

How I plan to use it in my business:

_____

_____

_____

_____

_____

_____

Who I'll share this idea with:

_____

_____

Idea 3:

_____

_____

_____

_____

_____

_____

How I plan to use it in my business:

_____

_____

_____

_____

_____

_____

Who I'll share this idea with:

_____

_____

Irresistible Customer-Relationship Model

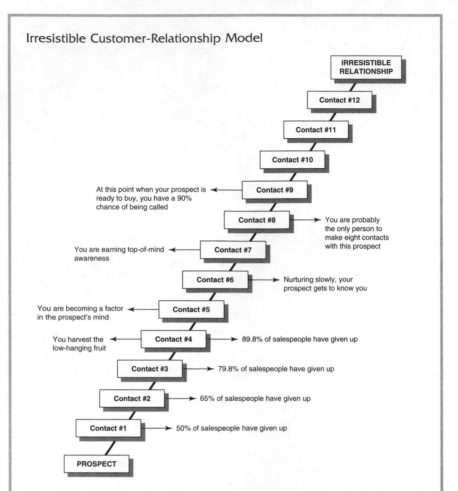

Note: This chart is based on the findings of major national marketing research firms.

Inform and Compel Your Prospects to Want to Meet with You

Sample Letter 1

BIG INSURANCE COMPANY
123 Main Street
Your Town, ST 12121
(555) 555-5555

Date

Susan Johnson
456 Elm Avenue
Your Town, ST 12456

Dear Mrs. Johnson:

Welcome to your new home. Now might be a good time to consider reviewing your insurance policies.

This is especially important if you're not already insured with Big Insurance Company. As a Big Insurance Company agent, I can handle all your insurance needs.

In a few days, I'll contact you with a special gift—a Big Insurance Company Road Atlas. You can contact me at 555-5555, or return the attached tear-off reply if you need to reach me before then.

Sincerely,
Frank Thompson, CLU, LUTC
President

Information Checklist

I'd also like information on:

- ❑ Auto insurance
- ❑ Homeowners insurance
- ❑ Health insurance
- ❑ Review of my insurance file
- ❑ Car financing
- ❑ Other_____

YES . . . I'd like to know more about Big Insurance Company's insurance review.

Please call me at

_____

Best time to call

_____

(Continued)

Susan Johnson
456 Elm Avenue
Your Town, ST 12456

ATTENTION: Frank Thompson
Big Insurance Company
P.O. Box 555
Midwestern Town, IL 20202

Sequential Letter 1

Hi, Susan . . . as you can see, I've attached a nice, crisp "million dollar bill" to the top of this letter. And, I've done it for three reasons:

1. Because you've just moved into the area, you're now one of my neighbors, and hopefully will become one of my friends. And because good friends are hard to come by, when you find one, they're worth a million.

2. What I have to say is very important to say, and I wanted to catch your attention.

3. Finally, my message has to do with money—a *lot* of money—and this "million dollar bill" is representative of a goal that we can achieve by working together.

Most people who live in this area, over their working lifetime, will earn well over a million dollars. The steps you take now, with your insurance coverage can mean the difference between losing it all, protecting it with safety and security, or maximizing and enhancing its value.

One of the biggest challenges people face when moving to a new area, is who to trust to handle their needs. If they make the wrong choice, it could be devastating for them and their family's future security.

If they make the right choice, they can not only be assured of getting the best value for their insurance dollar, but they can rest easily knowing that they are appreciated, well taken care of, and are enjoying a refreshingly fun and enjoyable business relationship.

It's no wonder why so many of your neighbors choose to do business with our agency. If you'd like to know more about why they're so happy with our service, I invite you to contact Sheila, my Office Manager, to arrange a time that we can get together. It typically only takes about 17 minutes.

So, please call Sheila right away . . . I know you're going to be pleased.

Your Name

P.S. I'm so confident that our time will be well spent, and that I can show you some solid reasons to do business with my agency, that I'll bring along a $25.00 blank check. If you don't agree that our meeting provided valuable information to you (regardless of whether or not we end up doing business together), I'll let you fill in the name of your favorite charity, and I'll make the donation in your name.

Your Insurance Agency
Your Name, Agent
123 Main Street, Your Town, State Zip
Voice: (000) 000-0000 Fax: (000) 000-0000
E-mail: agents name@yourname.com
web site: www.agentsname.com

Sequential Letter 2

Hi, Susan. . . . It's me again. Remember, I'm the one who sent you the "million dollar bill" a few days ago.

My last letter talked about *big* money . . . how to protect your valuable assets from sudden and unexpected loss, and at the same time, benefit from a fun and refreshingly enjoyable business relationship (something that's sorely missing in too many businesses today).

Because I haven't heard from you yet, I thought I'd attach a real **one-dollar bill,** and talk to you for a moment about *real* money . . . the kind of money that inadvertently slips through most people's hands every day.

I'm going to be right up front with you, and let you know that in actuality, there is really very little difference in most insurance

(Continued)

policies from one insurance company to another. The real difference (and where most people waste thousands of dollars), is in the types and amounts of coverage they purchase, and the agent and agency they choose to handle their insurance needs.

If you'll take just a minute to give Sheila, my Office Manager, a call, she'll help find a time that's convenient for us to get together so I can show you why so many of your neighbors choose us to help them not only make smart *real* money decisions, but *big* money decisions, as well.

As I mentioned in my last letter, I know your time will be well invested.

Looking forward to seeing you soon,

Your Name

P.S. Remember what I said in my last letter: I'm so confident that our time will be well spent, and that I can show you some solid reasons to do business with my agency, that I'll bring along a $25.00 blank check. If you don't agree that our meeting provided valuable information to you (regardless of whether or not we end up doing business together), I'll let you fill in the name of your favorite charity, and I'll make the donation in your name.

Your Insurance Agency
Your Name, Agent
123 Main Street, Your Town, State Zip
Voice: (000) 000-0000 Fax: (000) 000-0000
E-mail: agents name@yourname.com
web site: www.agentsname.com

Sequential Letter 3

Hi, Susan . . .

Yep, it's me again . . . the person who's trying to save you *real big* money by making sure your insurance policies are up to date, that you're not paying for coverage that you don't need, and that you're getting the best value for your insurance dollar possible.

By now, you've no doubt noticed that the amount of money that's attached to the top of each letter is getting smaller. In fact, this letter only has a quarter attached to it.

Know what else is getting smaller with the passage of time?

Actually, a couple of things . . .

1. The amount of money you may save by failing to get together with me.

2. The mental peace and security you'll have, not knowing for sure if you're carrying the right coverages on your insurance policies.

Really, it only takes a few minutes for me to look over your policies and give you that all-important second opinion . . . you know, the one that will either confirm that you're okay (in which case, you can rest easy). Or, point out a couple of areas that you may want to consider changing or updating.

Please give Sheila, my Office Manager, a call. She'll be glad to find a time that's convenient for us to get together so I can show how to keep your hard-earned money from slipping through your hands.

As I mentioned in my last letter, I know your time will be well invested.

Looking forward to seeing you soon,

Your Name

P.S. Remember what I said in my last letter: I'm so confident that our time will be well spent, and that I can show you some solid reasons to do business with my agency, that I'll bring along a $25.00 blank check. If you don't agree that our meeting provided valuable information to you (regardless of whether or not we end up doing business together), I'll let you fill in the name of your favorite charity, and I'll make the donation in your name.

Your Insurance Agency
Your Name, Agent
123 Main Street, Your Town, State Zip
Voice: (000) 000-0000 Fax: (000) 000-0000
E-mail: agents name@yourname.com
web site: www.agentsname.com

Sequential Letter 4

Susan . . .

Just thought I'd get my two cents in one more time.

Any more, most people won't bother to bend over to pick up a couple of pennies.

(Continued)

I know it doesn't seem like much, but getting two cents worth of advice from someone who's helped so many your neighbors save *real big* money on their insurance, and/or better protect their valuable assets and future earnings from loss, can be one of the most cents-able things you can do.

Let's get together soon. Please give Sheila, my Office Manager, a call. She'll be glad to find a time that's convenient for us to get together so I can show how to keep your hard-earned money from slipping through your hands.

As I mentioned in my last letter, I know your time will be well invested.

Looking forward to seeing you soon,

Your Name

P.S. Remember what I said in my last letter: I'm so confident that our time will be well spent, and that I can show you some solid reasons to do business with my agency, that I'll bring along a $25.00 blank check. If you don't agree that our meeting provided valuable information to you (regardless of whether or not we end up doing business together), I'll let you fill in the name of your favorite charity, and I'll make the donation in your name.

Your Insurance Agency
Your Name, Agent
123 Main Street, Your Town, State Zip
Voice: (000) 000-0000 Fax: (000) 000-0000
E-mail: agents name@yourname.com
web site: www.agentsname.com

Sequential Letter 5

Susan . . .

I know what you're thinking . . . "What? No money?!"

Nope. Not this time.

Instead, I'm giving you an apology and a small packet of Tylenol tablets.

Why am I doing this?

Well, the apology is because in my last four letters to you, I've tried my darnedest to help you see the value in meeting with me to review your insurance policies . . . but somehow, I haven't succeeded.

The Tylenol tablets are to relieve the stress and giant headache from not knowing for sure if you're properly covered and are getting the best value possible for your insurance dollar.

Of course, there is a better, more permanent way to relieve the stress.

You already know what that is . . .

Just give Sheila, my Office Manager, a call. She'll be glad to find a time that's convenient for us to get together so I can show how to keep your hard-earned money from slipping through your hands.

Believe me, Susan, I wouldn't keep writing to you if I didn't know for sure that your time will be well invested.

The longer you wait, the longer you delay getting the same protection, savings, comfort, and peace of mind so many of your neighbors are getting. So why not pick up the phone and give us a call . . . I know it will be in your best interest.

Your Name

P.S. Don't forget my promise: I'm so confident that our time will be well spent, and that I can show you some solid reasons to do business with my agency, that I'll bring along a $25.00 blank check. If you don't agree that our meeting provided valuable information to you (regardless of whether or not we end up doing business together), I'll let you fill in the name of your favorite charity, and I'll make the donation in your name.

Your Insurance Agency
Your Name, Agent
123 Main Street, Your Town, State Zip
Voice: (000) 000-0000 Fax: (000) 000-0000
E-mail: agents name@yourname.com
web site: www.agentsname.com

THE LIFETIME VALUE OF A HYPOTHETICAL CUSTOMER

		Hypothetical Business	10% Increase
A	Monthly leads	100	110

(Continued)

		Hypothetical Business	10% Increase
B	Annual leads (A×12)	1200	1320
C	Conversion rate (%)	30%	33%
D	Number of new customers annually (B×C)	360	436
E	Average $ amount of each sale	$100	$110
F	Profit margin (%)	50%	55%
G	Profit per sale (E×F)	$50	$61
H	Average number of purchases per year per customer	2	2.2
I	Profit per year per customer (G×H)	$100	$133
J	Average number of years customer buys from you	3	3.3
K	**Lifetime profit value of each customer (I×J)**	$300	$439
L	Lifetime profit value for all customers (D×K)	$108,000	$191,329
M	Number of referrals from customer during lifetime	1	1.1
N	Referral conversion rate (%)	50%	55%
O	Number of referrals per customer (M×N)	0.5	0.605
P	Total number of referrals during lifetime (D×O)	180	264
R	Lifetime profit from referrals (K×P)	$54,000	$115,754
S	**Total lifetime profit value of each customer (K+(K×O))**	$450	$705

T	Total lifetime profit value for all new customers (L+R)	$162,000	$307,082

	Percentage increase		89.56%
	Lifetime $ value of each new lead	$135	$233
	Value of each new lead (% increase)		72.32%
	Lifetime $ value of each new client	$450	$705
	Value of each new customer (% increase)		56.66%

THE LIFETIME VALUE OF YOUR AVERAGE CUSTOMER

		Your Business	Percent Increase	New Figures
A	Monthly leads		%	
B	Annual leads (A×12)			
C	Conversion rate (%)		%	%
D	Number of new customers annually (B×C)			
E	Average $ amount of each sale	$	%	$
F	Profit margin (%)		%	%
G	Profit per sale (E×F)	$		$
H	Average number of purchases per year per customer		%	
I	Profit per year per customer (G×H)	$		$
J	Average number of years customer buys from you		%	
K	**Lifetime profit value of each customer (I×J)**	$		$

(*Continued*)

		Your Business	Percent Increase	New Figures
L	Lifetime profit value for all customers (D×K)			
M	Number of referrals from customer during lifetime		%	
N	Referral conversion rate (%)		%	%
O	Number of referrals per customer (M×N)			
P	Total number of referrals during lifetime (D×O)			
R	Lifetime profit from referrals (K×P)	$		$
S	**Total lifetime profit value of each customer (K+(K×O))**	$		$
T	Total lifetime profit value for all new customers (L + R)	$		$
	Percentage increase			%
	Lifetime $ value of each new lead	$		$
	Value of each new lead (% increase)			%
	Lifetime $ value of each new client	$		$
	Value of each new customer (% increase)			%

AD RESPONSE/COST ANALYSIS

Cost of Ad ($)	Number of Responses	Cost per Response ($)	Cost to Run Ad ($)
1,000	5	200	1,000
1,000	50	20	1,000
1,000	500	2	1,000

AD PROFITABILITY/COST ANALYSIS

Cost of Ad ($)	Amount of Sales ($)	Sales To Break Even	Cost to Run Ad ($)
1,000	50	20	1,000
1,000	500	2	1,000
1,000	5,000	.2	1,000

A $1,000 ad, promotion or marketing campaign costs the same to run whether it pulls 5 responses, 50 responses, or 500 responses.

And if you earn $50, $500 or $5,000 from that ad, it still cost you $1,000 to run.

You must carefully track and analyze all your marketing efforts and continually try to improve their effectiveness.

Advertising and Promotion Results Analysis		
A	Date the ad or promotion ran or letters sent out	
B	Promotion name	
C	Ad code	
D	Targeted market	
E	Number of letters sent	
F	Number of responses and percent of response	Number Percentage
G	Number of sales	
H	Sale value	
	Price per unit ___ × number of sales: ___	
I	Less cost of fulfillment *(packaging, product, shipping, etc.)*	
J	Less cost of promotion or ad	

(Continued)

Advertising and Promotion Results Analysis	
Number of letters: ___ × stamp/letter: ___ =	_____
Printing of letters/unit: ___	
Envelopes: ___ × number of letters: ___	
Stuffing envelopes (labor): ___	
Grabber/unit: ___ × number of letters: ___ =	_____
K	Net profit (loss) on promotion *(Total sales less cost of promotion and cost of fulfillment)*	
L	Profit-loss per $ spent on promotion *(Divide net profit-loss by cost of promotion)*	

Action Plan

A well-known philosopher once said, "Ideas are like slippery fish. Unless you capture them with the point of a pen or pencil, they'll slip away never to be seen again." But, merely capturing is not enough. Unless you actually do something with either the fish or the idea, neither will be of much value to you.

Use this page to record the best ideas you got from this section, how you plan to implement them in your business, and who you'll share the ideas with. Reliable studies clearly demonstrate that if you teach or share with someone an idea you've learned, your personal understanding and retention of that idea are dramatically enhanced.

Idea 1:

_____
_____
_____
_____
_____
_____

How I plan to use it in my business:

_____

_____
_____
_____
_____
_____

Who I'll share this idea with:

_____
_____

Idea 2:

_____
_____
_____
_____
_____

How I plan to use it in my business:

_____
_____
_____
_____
_____

Who I'll share this idea with:

_____
_____

Idea 3:

_____
_____
_____
_____
_____

How I plan to use it in my business:

_____
_____

_____
_____
_____
_____

Who I'll share this idea with:

_____
_____

How to Get More Money from Each Sale

1. Bumping or Up-Selling

What can I do to sell more of the same product or service that my customer is buying?

_____
_____
_____
_____
_____
_____

2. Cross-Selling or Add-Ons

What additional items can I logically add on to my customer's purchases that will enhance the benefits they gain from their original purchase?

_____
_____
_____
_____
_____

3. Packaging or Bundling

What complimentary products can I bundle together that will increase the total value of the sale, but cost my customers less than if purchased separately?

_____
_____
_____
_____

_____

_____

4. Point-of-Purchase Promotions

What specific items, products or services would make good impulse purchases that I could offer at the time of the sale?

_____

_____

_____

_____

_____

_____

5. Payment Plans

What kind of payment options can I offer that focus on monthly payments, rather than the total amount of the sale?

_____

_____

_____

_____

_____

_____

6. Raise Your Prices

What can I do to raise my prices and still remain the best value for my customers?

_____

_____

_____

_____

_____

_____

7. Change the "Profile" of Your Average Customer

What can I do to "upgrade" my average customer, so I can deal with a more affluent, more "sophisticated" buyer, and compete on issues other than low price?

_____

_____

_____

_____
_____
_____

What can I do to downgrade the profile of my average customer, so I can attract a greater volume of customers?

_____
_____
_____
_____
_____
_____

8. Offer Continuity Programs

What kinds of programs can I develop that will enable me to provide an on-going service, or automatically deliver products and charge their account or credit card each month?

_____
_____
_____
_____
_____
_____

9. Offer Subscriptions

What can I offer where my customers pay up-front and receive the products or services month-to-month?

_____
_____
_____
_____
_____
_____

10. Give Your Customers a Choice

What kinds of products or services can I offer my customers that would provide a choice between a low-end (cheap), middle (desired sale), and high-end (expensive)?

_____
_____

_____
_____
_____
_____

11. Until Further Notice

What can I offer my customers that will allow me to automatically send previously selected products or services on a regular basis, and automatically charge their credit cards, unless they specifically ask me to stop?

_____
_____
_____
_____
_____
_____

12. Reverse the Risk

Whenever any sale is made, someone is being asked to assume the risk. How can I take the risk of buying my products and services away from my customers?

_____
_____
_____
_____
_____
_____

13. Acquire Customers at Break-Even and Make the Profits on the Back-End

What strategies can I employ, or offers can I make that will allow me to acquire new customers at break-even (or even a loss), and make my profits on back-end products or repeat business?

_____
_____
_____
_____
_____

What additional no-cost or low-cost things can I add to the sale that have a high perceived value to the customer, and that might encourage him or her to purchase?

_____
_____
_____
_____
_____
_____

How to Get Your Customers to Buy More Often

1. Capture the Names and Addresses of All Prospects, Customers, and Visitors

The most valuable asset in my business is my mailing list of people who have purchased from me before, or who may have shown any interest, whatsoever, in my business or the products or services I offer. How can I effectively capture their contact information?

_____
_____
_____
_____
_____
_____

2. Ask Your Customers to Buy from You Again

How can I use my customer database to get people to buy from me again?

_____
_____
_____
_____
_____
_____

3. Develop a Strong Back-End

What additional items can I sell to my existing customers subsequent to their original purchase that would add to the benefits they enjoy from that purchase, and that would enhance their lives or their business?

_____

_____

_____

_____

_____

_____

4. Make Doing Business with You Fun

How can I make it enjoyable for my customers to do business with me?

_____

_____

_____

_____

_____

5. Hold Special, Preferred Customers Events and Sales

What can I do to show my best customers that I appreciate them and their loyalty?

_____

_____

_____

_____

_____

6. Set up Joint-Ventures with Other, Complimentary-But-Non-Competing Companies

Which other companies have products or services that would naturally compliment what I offer but don't carry, that would provide additional benefits or enhancements to my customers?

_____

_____

_____

_____

_____

7. Program Your Clients for Repeat Purchases

What can I do to encourage my customers to buy from me again (frequent purchase programs)?

_____

_____

_____

_____

_____

_____

Extend Your Customers' Average Buying Lifetime

1. Communicate Regularly with Your Current Customers

How can I best keep in touch with my customers and let them know of special events, sales, promotions, and so on?

_____

_____

_____

_____

_____

_____

2. Contact Inactive Customers

What can I do to encourage those customers who haven't purchased recently to buy from me again?

_____

_____

_____

_____

_____

_____

3. Promise a Lot . . . Deliver Even More

How can I increase my service and the attention I give to my customers so that becomes one of my major competitive advantages?

_____

_____

_____

_____

_____

_____

4. Show Appreciation to Your Customers

How can I best show my customers that I care about them and appreciate their business, and that I don't consider them "just another sale?"

_____

_____

_____

_____

_____

_____

5. EARN the Right to Their Continued Business

Earn—What can I do to show my customers that I am worthy of their continued business?

_____

_____

_____

_____

_____

Ask—How can I effectively ask them to do business with me without appearing to beg for their business?

_____

_____

_____

_____

_____

Recognize and _Reward_—What can I do to continually let my customers know I appreciate them and their continued support?

_____

_____

_____

_____

_____

_____

Next—What other things can I do to solidify our relationship and in effect, obligate my customers to me?

_____

_____

_____

_____

_____

_____

Sample Thank You Letter 1

LMNOP Insurance Agency
123 Main Street
Your Town, ST 12121
(555) 555-5555

Date
Susan Johnson
456 Elm Avenue
Your Town, ST 12456

Dear Susan:

I would like to take this opportunity to thank you for choosing me to be your personal insurance specialist.

I have enjoyed filling your needs for your life insurance.

If there's anything further I can do for you, please don't hesitate to call on me.

Sincerely,
Frank Thompson, CLU, LUTC
President

Sample Thank You Letter 2

LMNOP Insurance Agency
   123 Main Street
   Your Town, ST 12121
   (555) 555-5555

Date
Susan Johnson
456 Elm Avenue
Your Town, ST 12456

Dear Policyholder:
Thanks, Susan . . . your business, trust, and confidence is very much appreciated!

There's no question that you have a number of choices when it comes to who handles your insurance needs . . . and we're honored that you chose our agency.

Our commitment to you is simple, Susan . . .

1. To be available when you need us;
2. To keep you informed of changes in policies, coverages, or laws as they might affect you;
3. To give you the opportunity to review and update your policies at least annually
4. To make you aware of additional policies or coverages that may be of benefit to you; and
5. To see that you are getting the best value for your insurance dollar.

In short Susan, we want to be a very important part of your financial team . . . always making sure that you're well taken care of and that we're here and available when you need us.

To further show my appreciation for your decision to do business with us, I've enclosed a special report that I thought might be of interest to you. It's called, "How to Turn a Single Sale into a Million Dollar Business."

(Continued)

In this report you'll find several ideas that can help give your business a boost in these highly competitive times.

Once again Susan, thanks for the confidence you placed in us . . . and remember that we're here and committed to helping you. If you have any questions or concerns about your policy or coverages, please feel free to give us a call. We're anxious to be of assistance to you.

Agent's Name

P.S. If you have any questions about the enclosed report, or would like additional information or articles, please feel free to call me personally.

Your Insurance Agency
Your Name, Agent
123 Main Street, Your Town, State Zip
Voice: (000) 000-0000 Fax: (000) 000-0000
E-mail: agents name@youmame.com
web site: www.agentsname.com

27 POINT BUSINESS CHECKLIST

		Good	Fair	Poor
1	Is the outside of your store/office/ place of business clean and inviting (including landscaping, parking, and walkways)?			
2	Are the windows and doors clean, attractive, and inviting?			
3	Are your walls clean and painted, especially around light switches, door jambs, and door handles?			
4	Are the sidewalks and entrances clean and free of debris and trash?			
5	Are your desks, countertops and shelves dusted, neat, and tidy?			

6	Is the temperature comfortable for the people working there as well as visitors?			
7	Are there any unpleasant or detractive odors?			
8	Are your products displayed attractively and invitingly?			
9	Are all items priced, with the price tag carefully placed and easily locatable?			
10	Are your staff helpful, friendly, knowledgeable, and enthusiastic?			
11	Do your staff always put your customers above everything else?			
12	Are your stock levels sufficient to ensure that your customers' never have to leave empty handed?			
13	Can you get out of stock items quickly enough to ensure that your customer won't purchase from another vendor or supplier?			
14	Do you deliver back ordered or out of stock items to save your customers another trip to your business?			
15	When put on hold, will your customers have to wait long or be transferred to another employee to get the information they're requesting?			

(*Continued*)

		Good	Fair	Poor
16	Do all your staff always greet every customer with a genuine smile and greeting whether a face to face meeting or a telephone call?			
17	Do all your staff show genuine, helpful interest to every customer?			
18	Do all your staff make contact and listen attentively to every customer's needs?			
19	Do each of your employees demonstrate a genuine serving attitude?			
20	Do you respond to every request by sending information out the same day by first class mail?			
21	Is your reception area clean, uncluttered, and present a professional and organized appearance?			
22	Are your chairs comfortable and the tables stable and not wobbly?			
23	If you serve refreshments, are your glasses, plates, and utensils clean and free from spots or blemishes?			
24	Do your staff dress appropriately for the business they work in, the job they do, and the customers they serve?			

25	Do your staff thoroughly and author-itatively know what they're selling? Have they use it, experienced it, eaten it, work it, traveled in it?			
26	Do you and your staff go the extra mile to please, help and astonish your customers?			
27	Are your customer and employee rest rooms always kept as clean, fresh and comfortable as you keep yours at home?			

Action Plan

A well-known philosopher once said, "Ideas are like slippery fish. Unless you capture them with the point of a pen or pencil, they'll slip away never to be seen again." But, merely capturing is not enough. Unless you actually do something with either the fish or the idea, neither will be of much value to you.

Use this page to record the best ideas you got from this section, how you plan to implement them, your business, and who you'll share the ideas with. Reliable studies clearly demonstrate that if you teach or share with someone an idea you've learned, your personal understanding and retention of that idea are dramatically enhanced.

Idea 1:

_____

_____

_____

_____

_____

_____

How I plan to use it in my business:

_____

_____

_____

_____

Who I'll share this idea with:

_____

_____

Idea 2:

_____

_____

_____

_____

_____

_____

How I plan to use it in my business:

_____

_____

_____

_____

_____

Who I'll share this idea with:

_____

_____

Idea 3:

_____

_____

_____

_____

_____

_____

How I plan to use it in my business:

_____

_____

_____

_____

_____

Who I'll share this idea with:

_____

_____

Million-Dollar Case Studies

Imagine opening your mailbox to discover a gold bar inside or a shoeshine kit or even a piggy bank. Wouldn't you be eager to open this unusual package? You'll even keep something that's useful or especially clever.

It's no secret that direct-mail programs cost money. But *effective* programs are based not only on the unique quality of the delivery but also on the effectiveness of the accompanying message. And they don't have to be expensive.

The following section details some of our most effective promotions including the proven sales letter that accompanied each mailing.

Aspirin Pack Mailer

Foreclosure Headaches?

I can give you more than just aspirin!

Dear [prospective client]

Lenders take advantage of people every day. Don't let it happen to you. Our *free report* helps homeowners fight back and get the cash they need.

If you think you might be in foreclosure read this immediately!

Free report: How to Stop Foreclosure and Get Cash Fast

Learn how to:

- Sell your house.
- Get a cash loan.

(Continued)

- Refinance your home.
- Save your home and equity.

Good people fall behind in their payments for many reasons. Whether it's job loss, divorce, or unexpected setbacks, you are not alone!

Call this *free* recording 24 hours a day and get your *free report: How to Stop Foreclosure and Get Cash Fast*

Call: 800-XXX-XXXX today!

Here's the good news. Home Savers, LLC can reveal the secret to stopping foreclosure and get you the cash you need . . . fast. Just call the *free*, prerecorded number 24 hours a day and get your free report: *How to Sell Your Home and Get the Cash You Need.*

Call: 800-XXX-XXXX today.

Sincerely,

[your name]

P.S. There is an enormous cost if you don't act now. It's called "The cost of waiting." The longer you delay, the worse your problems become. But if you pick up the phone now and call 800-XXX-XXXX, you can learn the solution *to getting out of foreclosure* before it's too late. Get your *no risk or obligation* consumer information kit today!

Bank Bag Mailer

At last, an offer you can actually take to the bank!

Make more money with this simple business review than any other offer you've ever received or I'll pay you $50 cash!

Dear [personalized]:

One lovely spring morning many years ago, two young men graduated from the same college. They shared a lot in common. Both were intelligent with good grades, both were imaginative and resourceful, and both—as most young college graduates—were filled with grand and ambitious dreams of the future.

When these men returned to college for their 20th reunion, they still shared a lot in common. They were happily married with three children each. And both, coincidentally, had gone to work for the same corporation after graduation and were still employed there.

But there was one distinct difference. One of the men was the manager of a small department in the company; and the other was the president.

WHAT MADE THE DIFFERENCE?

Haven't we all wondered what makes this kind of difference in people's lives? Is it ambition or talent? Is it that one person seeks success and the other doesn't?

No. The true difference is a person's ability to surround themselves with other people of great talent and ability, and to utilize those talents to achieve his or hers own goals.

That's why I'm writing to you today. According to my research, you qualify for our **Free Platinum Review**. What's more, I'll send you a **Free World Time Calculator** for taking the time.

What is the Platinum Review? It's the most powerful tool you will ever find for discovering:

- Hidden revenue streams (I will explain and analyze three commonly overlooked areas of income)

- Money lost (five key areas in which many businesses are neglected and lose substantial revenue)

- Innovative leverage points (six regions of strength in your business that are currently undeveloped)

This is a *free, no pressure, no risk* evaluation.

What makes a [consultant] like me give away this kind of assessment for *free?*

(Continued)

It's easy. Some people who take advantage of my Platinum Review go on to use my services. Some don't. But enough of you choose to benefit from the *free* offer to make it profitable for me. So go for it!

If you still have some hesitation, let me address your concerns. What about cost? I may not be the least expensive [consultant] in the area, but is working with the cheapest [consultant] always the best for achieving long-term objectives? Of course not. I can bring you value that you need for your business goals.

I guarantee my offer. I am so sure that I can instantly show you three areas with a minimum value of $1,000 (in savings or money making ideas) that I'll pay YOU if you believe that my review wasn't worth at least $1,000. Yes, I'll pay the charity of your choice $50 in cash. You can't lose!

Sincerely,

[Your Name]

P.S. Invest just a few minutes of your time and I'll give you both the Free Platinum Review and the World Time Cock Calculator. And I guarantee that you'll make at least $1,000 return on your investment of time with me or I'll pay $50 cash!

Attached you'll find testimonials from a number of my clients . . . people just like you who've already benefited from the profits from my review.

Message in a Bottle Mailer

How a message in a bottle can map out hidden profits in your business. Guaranteed!

Dear [personalized]:

About XXX ago I sent you an offer in a bank deposit bag. But I never heard from you! So now I'm sending you a message in a bottle.

What I have to tell you is so vital that I needed a way to make certain that this letter got your attention. I can show you how to achieve maximum [insert your benefit here] from your business. I thought a message in a bottle would really make my point.

I'll give you a *free* World Time Clock and Calculator just for meeting with me.

What if you were walking along the beach and a bottle washed up with a message in it. Would you pick it up? And what if the message included a map that showed where to find hidden profit centers for your business. Would you read it? Can you believe that most people wouldn't? They expect solutions to materialize without any outside help.

Well, the real world doesn't work that way. The way to achieve amazing profits is found in the little extras. And that's what I'm an expert at finding; those little extras that add up to enormous cost saving to improve your bottom line.

This little message in a bottle could actually be your map to success. Here's what it's all about. My specialty is showing people just like you how to:

- Save money.
- Improve your bottom line profit.
- Reduce stress.
- Improve [name an action].
- [Add your own unique benefit here].

Don't be concerned about getting stuck in a high-pressured sales pitch. And don't worry that great business ideas are too complex or expensive to execute.

I've been in business for XX years and I've seen how many [consultants] they're dispense what they think is worthwhile information that, in reality, doesn't work when it's put into practice.

You'll get solid [information, expertise] when you work with [name of your company]. You won't get a pushy sales pitch. You'll get information you can use service you can trust.

(Continued)

You've already qualified for a *free* Platinum Review Package and a *free* World Time Clock and Calculator.

What is the Platinum Review? It's the most powerful tool you will ever find for discovering:

- Hidden revenue streams (I will explain and analyze three commonly overlooked areas of income)

- Money lost (five key areas in which many businesses are neglected and lose substantial revenue)

- Innovative leverage points (six regions of strength in your business that are currently undeveloped)

This is a *free, no pressure, no risk* evaluation.

I guarantee my offer. I am so sure that I can instantly show you three areas with a minimum value of $1,000 (in savings or money making ideas) that I'll pay YOU if you believe that my review wasn't worth at least $1,000. Yes, I'll pay the charity of your choice $50 in cash. You can't lose!

And to show you that I value your time, I'm offering you this fabulous World Time Clock and Calculator just for meeting with me. As they say, "time is money," and I won't waste a minute. To receive your *free* Platinum Review and World Time Clock and Calculator, call me at XXX-XXXX.

Why not call today?

Sincerely,

[Your Name, Company Name]

P.S. I guarantee that you'll make at least $1,000 return on investment from my Platinum Review!

Trash Can Mailer

Alex Mandossian, marketing consultant, approached me regarding a client of his. This client, Cal Waste, was running into stiff competition with large waste haulers in the Bay Area of California. They had exhausted all sales and marketing techniques using multiple postcards and cold calls. They no longer could get in contact with the buyers of waste hauling services for the local companies. Alex turned to me for ideas. We came up with the trash can mailer as the solution. Results proved out with an 11 percent appointment ratio.

Caution:

Throwing this final letter away may be harmful to your success.

Just in case you've been throwing my letters in the trash, I wanted to do it for you this time.

You can still receive a *free* World Clock Calculator and Platinum Review!

Dear [name]:

What's really going on in your business? Are you staying ahead of the competition? Are you working too hard and not getting the results you want? Is your [insert your product or service here] the best it can be?

If everything is perfect and you're totally happy with the status quo, then

(Continued)

THROW THIS LETTER AWAY ... YOU DON'T NEED ME.

But if you'd like to improve your business's profitability, then contact me!

I can prove to you that my system is more efficient and cost effective than anything you've seen before. To prove it, I will give you a *free* Platinum Review Package and World Time Clock and Calculator. I will show you how the numbers stack up against my strategies.

Isn't the definition of insanity doing the same thing over and over and expecting different results? So if you're tired of the results you're getting, then you need to do something different!

Just accept my offer for a *free*, no obligation, Platinum Review. In just 10 minutes I'll show how you can be making at least $1,000 profit starting right now!

I'll show you how to:

- Save money.
- Improve your bottom line profit.
- Reduce stress.
- Improve [name an action].
- [Add your own unique benefit here].

There are no drawbacks. All you risk is 10 minutes of your time. I even guarantee that *if I can't find at least three ways to save you $1,000, I'll give $50 cash to your favorite charity.*

Don't worry about a high-pressure sales pitch. I hate them as much as you do. I just want the opportunity to show you how my program can benefit you and your business.

Call today! You can reach me at XXX-XXX-XXXX to receive your *free* Review and World Time Clock and Calculator.

Sincerely,

[Your Name, Company Name]

P.S. I guarantee that you'll make at least $1,000 return on investment from my Platinum Review! The gift of a FREE World Time Clock and Calculator is my way of thanking you to take the time.

Needle in a Haystack Mailer

Finding the right [professional or service] is like looking for a needle in a haystack! Until now! Let [your company name] solve all your [service] needs.

Dear [prospective client]:

A good [professional] is a real find. It's getting there that's the challenge. Where do you begin? When you need a new [professional], look no further.

[Name of your business] has been serving businesses such as yours since XXXX. With our years of experience and our professional and friendly staff, we can fulfill all your [service] needs.

I'm so sure that you'll be pleased with our services that I'll give you a *free* [gift] just for meeting with me. There's no risk, no obligation. Even if you don't choose my company for your [service] needs, the [gift] is still yours to keep.

Did I mention quality? We all know it's not just about the price. Sure, there may be [service] companies out there that charge less, but do they guarantee your satisfaction? That's what sets [your company name] apart from all the others. If you're not satisfied, we'll resolve the problem or refund your money.

(Continued)

[Insert testimonial here]

You've got nothing to lose and everything to gain! Just be one of the first XX to meet with and the [gift] is yours!

Call today at XXX-XXX-XXXX and let us be your [service] solution.

Sincerely,

[your name]

Lottery Ticket Mailer

It's better than winning the Lottery!

Well, maybe not quite as exciting. But you're still a winner!

Dear [prospective client]:

Don't gamble with your company's future. Come to [name of your company] for all your [name of service] needs. Not only do we offer top quality service and dependability, but we can probably save you money too.

How? We're one of the most efficient and experienced [name of service or profession] in the area. We won't play around with your time or money "experimenting" with your business. We already know our job and what we can do for you.

Let us help you:

- Xxx
- Xxx
- Xxx

But don't take our word for it. Read what we've done for people such as [name of previous client]:
[Insert quote/testimonial here.]
Go ahead and scratch off the enclosed lottery ticket. You're guaranteed to be a winner! And you'll stay ahead of the game by choosing [name of your company] as your [name of service]. Risk is part of the real lottery game, but not with [name of company]. We guarantee our [service, quality, etc.]. We know how vital good [name of service] is to your company.
To redeem your winning scratch-off ticket, call us at XXX-XXX-XXXX for your *free* [gift]. There's no obligation, you have nothing to lose!
Sincerely,
[your name]
P.S. Don't forget, call today!

Business Card Magnet Mailer

OPTIONAL POSTCARD FRONT

SMILE!
Dear Neighbor:
Did you? Smile, that is. Or were you embarrassed and self-conscious about your smile?
Do all your family portraits depict you with a half smile, or maybe just a lip smile so none of your teeth show? If you've always wanted a glowing smile but are bothered by the way your teeth look, then I can help you change your whole outlook on life!
I'm a board certified dentist specializing in reconstructive dentistry to improve:

- Malformed and crooked teeth
- Yellowing and staining
- Repair chips and damage

(Continued)

Be one of the first XX people to make an appointment for a free consultation and I will give you a *free* [gift] just for taking the time to meet with me. There's no catch, no hidden obligation.
Call: 800-XXX-XXXX today!

OPTIONAL POSTCARD BACK

John Smith
    Home Savers, LLC
    123 Main Street
    Anytown, CA 90000
    Dear Neighbor,
    Are you looking for a whole new you? You can have it with a whole new smile!
    Here's what one of my patients has to say:

"Dr. Smith . . ."
    Janie Jones

I've help Janie and hundreds like her to regain their confidence by giving them back their smiles. And I can do the same for you or someone you love.
    CALL: 800-XXX-XXXX today for your *free* consultation and receive a *free* [gift] just for stopping by!
    P.S. Financial plans are available.

Magnifying Glass Mailer

Before you make a decision, be sure to read the fine print!
NOT ALL [SERVICE] COMPANIES ARE ALIKE
Let [your company name] help you sort out your [service] needs.

Dear [prospective client]:

Take a close look at your company's bottom line. Is it really where you want it to be? We at [your company name] are in the business of helping companies just like yours achieve their full potential.

We're so sure we can help your company that we back it up with an offer for a *free* [gift], just for taking the time to meet with us.

Our specialty is showing businesses like yours how to:

- Save money.
- Improve your bottom line profit.
- Reduce your stress.
- Improve [name an action].
- [Add your own unique benefit here].

This isn't a high-pressured sales pitch. And I won't be throwing complex business ideas your way that are too expensive to execute.

What I am offering you is solid, dependable [name of service]. Did I mention quality? We all know it's not just about the price. Sure, there may be [service] companies out there that charge less, but do they guarantee your satisfaction? That's what sets [your company name] apart from all the others. If you're not satisfied, we'll resolve the problem or refund your money.

[Insert testimonial here.]

All you need to do to receive your *free* [gift] is to give us a call at XXX-XXX-XXXX and be one of the first XX people to set up an appointment. The *free* [gift] is yours to keep, whether or not you decide to use our services.

Sincerely,
[your name]
P.S. Call today, before it's too late!

Maze Pen Mailer

Don't get lost in a maze of confusion!

Let [name of your company] help you find a shortcut through the tangle of choices.

Dear [prospective client]:

In the confusing maze of [name your service here], what your business really needs is a clear leader. [Name of your business] is just that leader.

We have more than XX years of experience in the field of [name of profession]. And unlike many of our competitors, we're here to help you find real long-term solutions, not just quick fixes.

Our specialty is showing business like yours how to:

- [Name three or four specific advantages of your service]
- Xxx
- Xxx
- Xxx

We've helped hundreds of clients with businesses much like yours reach their [name a specific area such as financial, human resources, etc.] goals. Let us show you how we can help you reach your business objectives too.

[Insert customer testimonial here]

Why not find out for yourself? Give me just 10 minutes of your time and I'll show you what we can do for your business. And I'll even give you a *free* [gift] for taking the time to meet with me.

You won't get a high-pressured sales pitch. I hate those as much as you do. What you will get is solid, constructive information to advance your business goals.

Don't miss this opportunity. Call today at XXX-XXX-XXXX!

Sincerely,

[your name]

P.S. Only the first XX customers will receive a *free* [gift], so call now!

Buried Treasure Mailer

Find buried treasure . . . right in your own company!

I have the map to help you get there.

Dear [prospective client]:

If you were walking along the beach one morning and spied a bottle washed ashore, would you take a closer look? Would you pick it up? What if there was something in it, like a map leading you to a buried treasure?

Well, that's what this letter really is. I can map out for you how to dig up buried opportunities to make more money in your business. Hidden prospects to increase your profits that take just a little more effort than reading a treasure map.

Of course, in the real world we don't find real bottles on the beach with real treasure maps. But there are ways to achieve amazing profits is found in the little extras. And it's that's what I'm an expert at finding; those little extras that add up to enormous cost saving to improve your bottom line.

This little message in a bottle could actually be your map to success. Here's what it's all about. My specialty is showing people just like you how to:

- Save money.
- Improve your bottom line profit.
- Reduce your stress.

(*Continued*)

- Improve [name an action].
- [Add your own unique benefit here].

I'll even give you a *free* [gift] just for meeting with me.

This isn't a high-pressured sales pitch. And I won't be throwing complex business ideas your way that are too expensive to execute.

You've already qualified for a *free* Business Review Package and a *free* [gift].

What is the Business Review? It's the most powerful tool you will ever find for discovering:

- Hidden revenue streams (I will explain and analyze commonly overlooked areas of income)
- Money lost (key areas in which many businesses are neglected and lose substantial revenue)
- Innovative leverage points (areas of strength in your business that are currently undeveloped)

This is a *free, no pressure, no risk* evaluation.

I guarantee my offer. I am so sure that I can instantly show you three areas with a minimum value of $1,000 (in savings or money making ideas) that I'll pay YOU if you believe that my review wasn't worth at least $1,000. Yes, I'll pay the charity of your choice $25 in cash. You can't lose!

And to show you that I value your time, I'm offering you this fabulous [gift] just for meeting with me. As they say, "time is money," and I won't waste a minute. To receive your *free* Business Review and [gift], call me at XXX-XXXX.

Why not call today?

Sincerely,

[Your Name, Company Name]

P.S. I guarantee that you'll make at least $1,000 return on investment from my Business Review!

Message in a Bottle Mailer

Don't Be Left Stranded without a Holiday Caterer

Dear Friend,

We don't want you to be left stranded this holiday season without a caterer. That's why we're sending you this important message.

WARNING: DON'T HIRE A CATERER UNTIL YOU READ THIS

The difference between average and exceptional is in the details. When you're looking for excellence in a caterer, you need to know these small secrets of catering that can make all the difference in your event. Here's a list of questions that most caterers hope you'll never ask.

Portion Size: Will I be charged per person or by the batch? Make sure your guests don't receive tiny portions when you paid for full-sized ones.

Hidden Food Costs: Will you feed members in the band? The photographer? Restaurant staff assigned to my event?

No-Shows: If you have guests who can't make your event at the last minute, you don't want to pay for food they won't be eating. What's the cutoff for changing my guest count? What if additional guests come?

Staff Expenses: How will I be charged for staffing? Will I be charged for staffing by the hour or by the event? Are there additional charges for behind-the-scenes staff?

Liquor: The bar tab can be one of the quickest ways to sky-rocket your catering tab. Will I pay by the glass or by the bottle? What happens to the leftovers? Can I bring in my own alcohol?

Leftovers: Who gets the leftovers—me or the house? Ask if any unserved food can be wrapped to go.

Event Coordinators: Who will be my onsite event coordinator? Is it the person who helped me plan the event or someone else?

Fresh Should Mean Fresh: Many caterers say they use fresh ingredients but actually used canned and prepackaged substitutes to save time and money. Which would you rather have?

Rentals: Will tableware be china, glass, or plastic? May I see what dishes and glasses will actually be used at my event? Are there rental charges associated with the tableware? Smart caterers use the same forks for appetizers and desserts with a quick wash between courses.

Other Services: Will you oversee the rest of my party? Do you have particular florists, musicians, and decorators that I can or must use? Will you coordinate with them on my behalf?

(Continued)

These are important questions to ask before choosing your next caterer. And we'll gladly answer these and more—with the truth and only the truth.

Please call me at 555-123-4567 to schedule and appointment to discuss your event and receive a *free gift* when we get together. But hurry! Our holiday dates are filling up quickly.

Sincerely,

Joe Doe

Joe's Restaurant

P.S. Don't forget to ask for your *free gift* just for considering Joe's Restaurant.

Million-Dollar Bill Mailer

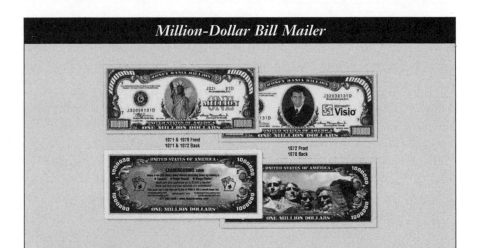

Feel like a million bucks!
Options:

- Thanks a million
- Feel like a million bucks
- Look like a million bucks
- Million-dollar inventory reduction

And look like it too!
Dear [prospective client]:
You know as well as anyone that when you look good you feel good too. And the reverse also holds true. When you feel good, you just naturally look it!

[Name of your company] can make you feel good. Good about the money you're saving by letting us [name of service]. Good about the peace of mind you have knowing that you can trust us to deliver [name of service] better than anyone.

We offer:

- XX years of experience
- Professional certification [name of certification]
- Money-back guarantee
- Save your company [money, time, reputation, etc.]
- Etc.

We're so sure you'll be thrilled with our [name of service], that we'll give you a *free* [gift] just for letting us meet with you. That's right! Just give us 10 minutes of your time and we'll give you a *free* [gift], yours to keep with no obligation.

Be one of the first XX callers to be part of this offer. Call today at XXX-XXX-XXXX to make an appointment. You have nothing to lose.

And you'll get more than a *free* [gift]. You'll get a [name of service] company that you can trust. We're dedicated to making you feel good about your decision to choose us as your [name of service/company].

Sincerely,

[your name]

P.S. Feel like a million bucks! Be one of the first XX callers to get your *free* [gift]. Call us today at XXX-XXX-XXXX.

Needle in a Haystack Mailer

Think That Finding Your Next Caterer Is like Searching for a Needle in a Haystack?

Dear Friend,

With so many choices of caterers for your next event, we know it's hard to search out the one that's right for you. Joe's Restaurant can end your search and make your next event a

(Continued)

resounding success. From menu selection to decorations, you'll receive personalized attention to detail guaranteed to make your event stand out.

Here's what some of our customers are saying about Joe's Restaurant . . .

> Our staff and guests all agree—this year's holiday party was the best ever! And we owe it all to you and your staff. The food was exquisite, the service impeccable and, best of all, we came in under our budget by nearly 20 percent! We look forward to working with you again and again!
> Kelly Dean
> Insurance Services, Inc.
> Woodland Hills, California
> Customer for seven years

Our experienced staff members are veterans at planning successful events for area businesses. Please call me at 555.123.4567 for a complimentary evaluation of your next event.
Sincerely,
Joe Doe
Joe's Restaurant

Piggy Bank Mailer

Here's advice you can bank on!

And you don't have to wait "until pigs can fly"!

Dear [prospective client]:

Have you ever passed on advice that, when you looked back, was advice that you wished you would have taken?

That's why I'm writing to you today. My advice can help you and your business make money. According to my research, you qualify for our *free* Business Review. What's more, I'll send you a *free* [gift] for taking the time to meet with me.

What is my Business Review? It's the most powerful tool you will ever find for discovering:

- Hidden revenue streams (I will explain and analyze commonly overlooked areas of income)
- Money lost (key areas in which many businesses are neglected and lose substantial revenue)
- Innovative leverage points (areas of strength in your business that are currently undeveloped)

This is a *free, no pressure, no risk* evaluation.

What makes a [consultant] like me give away this kind of assessment for *free?*

It's easy. Some people who take advantage of my Business Review go on to use my services. Some don't. But enough of you choose to benefit from the *free* offer to make it profitable for me. So go for it! Don't be concerned about getting stuck in a high-pressured sales pitch. And don't worry that great business ideas are too complex or expensive to execute.

I've been in business for XX years and I've seen how many [consultants] they're dispense what they think is worthwhile information that, in reality, doesn't work when it's put into practice.

You'll get solid [information, expertise] when you work with [name of your company]. You won't get a pushy sales pitch. You'll get information you can use service you can trust.

I may not be the least expensive [consultant] in the area, but is working with the lowest priced [consultant] always the best for achieving your goals? Of course not. I can bring you value that you need for your business objectives.

I guarantee my offer. I am so sure that I can instantly show you three areas with a minimum value of $1,000 (in savings or money making

(*Continued*)

ideas) that I'll pay YOU if you believe that my review wasn't worth at least $1,000. Yes, I'll pay the charity of your choice $25 in cash. You can't lose!

Sincerely,

[Your Name]

P.S. Invest just a few minutes of your time and I'll give you both the *free* Business Review and the [gift]. And I guarantee that you'll make at least $1,000 return on your investment of time with me or I'll pay $25 cash!

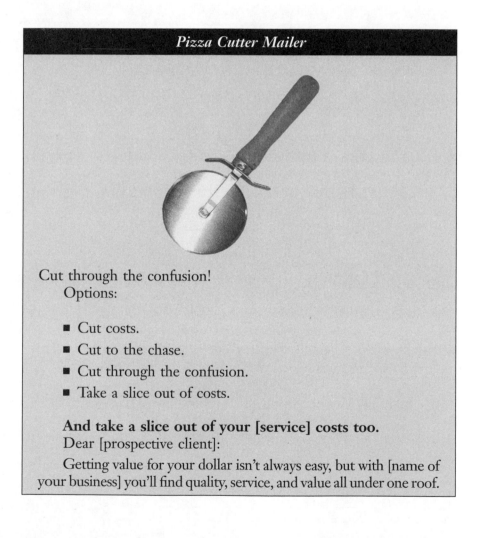

Pizza Cutter Mailer

Cut through the confusion!
Options:

- Cut costs.
- Cut to the chase.
- Cut through the confusion.
- Take a slice out of costs.

And take a slice out of your [service] costs too.
Dear [prospective client]:

Getting value for your dollar isn't always easy, but with [name of your business] you'll find quality, service, and value all under one roof.

To show you what I mean, I'm offering a *free* [service, or consultation] and a *free pizza*, too!

What if I could show you ways to cut your costs of [service] in a manageable piece? Yes, I can save you money on [service]. Just call for your *free* consultation at XXX-XXX-XXXX. There's no risk, no obligation. Best of all, you'll walk away with a coupon for a *free* pizza on me.

Ours is the [name of service] of choice for businesses in [name of city] because we:

[state specific attributes and benefits such as the following]

- Save you money.
- Show you how to be more efficient.
- Establish a consistent plan.
- Offer quality.

What are our customers saying about our [service]?
[testimonials here]

You be the judge! Call today to find out what we can do for your business too.

Sincerely,

[your name]

P.S. Act now while this offer is hot. Call today and get a coupon for a *free* pizza!

Ice Cream Scoop Mailer

(Continued)

What's the Scoop?

Have you heard the latest?

Dear [prospective client]:

We sent you an ice cream scooper and a coupon for some frozen treats just to give you the latest scoop on [name of your company]!

[your company name] now offers [new service, new personnel, etc.]

(Write one or two paragraphs about the latest achievement or happening at your company, such as: moved to new location, hired a new director, joined forces with another company, won an award, offering a new service/ product, etc.)

What does this mean to you? Now [your company name] can bring you:

[insert specific benefits for your clients]

- Save money.
- Improve your bottom line profit.
- Reduce your stress.

We're so sure you'll be thrilled with our new [name of service], that we'll give you a *free* [gift] just for letting us meet with you to tell you about it. That's right! Just give us 10 minutes of your time and we'll give you a *free* [gift], yours to keep with no obligation. Because you deserve a treat!

Be one of the first XX callers to be part of this offer. Call today at XXX-XXX-XXXX to make an appointment. There's no high-pressured sales pitch. We don't have to. If our new [service] is just what you need, you'd be crazy not to take us up on the offer.

We're waiting for your call!

Sincerely,

[your name]

P.S. Call right away to be one of the first eligible for a *free* [gift]. Time is running out!

Seed Packet Mailer

Start Growing Your Business Today!
Let [your company name] show you how.
Dear [prospective client]:
We know money doesn't grow on trees. But what does it take for a business to grow? Saving money is one way.

We at [name of your company] can help you save money the smart way by cutting your [name of service] costs. Yet, cutting costs doesn't have to mean cutting corners too.

By choosing [name of your company] to handle all your [name of service] needs, we can save you time and frustration so you can concentrate on other areas of your business. And we can take care of your little [name of service] problems before they have a chance to grow into big ones.

Why choose [name of your company]?

[list benefits to client here, such as quality, timeliness, years in business, guaranteed satisfaction, etc.]

- Xxx
- Xxx
- Xxx
- Xxx

(Continued)

If you're willing to invest just a few minutes of your time right now, we'll make it worth your while. Be one of the first XX callers to book a *free*, no-obligation assessment and you'll receive a *free* [gift]! Even if you decide not to select our [name of service] services, the gift is yours to keep, free!

Call XXX-XXX-XXXX today, before it's too late!

Sincerely,

[your name]

P.S. This is a no hassle, no risk, no hard-sell assessment. Let us show you how we can help your business today!

Silver Platter Mailer

An Invitation to You on a Silver Platter

Dear Friend,

At Joe's Restaurant, we make your catering event so simple that we practically deliver it on a silver platter. From menu selection to decorations, you'll receive white-gloved treatments guaranteed to make your event a success.

Here's what some of our customers are saying about Joe's Restaurant . . .

> Our staff and guests all agree—this year's holiday party was the best ever! And we owe it all to you and your staff. The food was exquisite, the service impeccable and, best of all, we came in under our budget by nearly 20 percent! We look forward to working with you again and again!
> Kelly Dean

Insurance Services, Inc.
Woodland Hills, California
Customer for seven years

Our experienced staff members are veterans at planning successful events for area businesses. Please call me at 555.123.4567 for a complimentary evaluation of your next event.
Sincerely,
Joe Doe
Joe's Restaurant

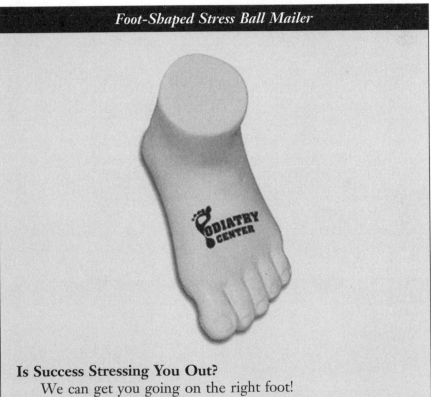

Foot-Shaped Stress Ball Mailer

Is Success Stressing You Out?
We can get you going on the right foot!
Dear [prospective client]:
Do you find yourself working harder and longer and still not catching up? Are you overwhelmed by the enormous responsibilities of running a successful business?

(Continued)

Wouldn't you rather be working smarter instead of working harder?

Don't feel trapped. There is a way out! We can reduce your [name of service or industry] stress almost immediately and still keep you a step ahead of your competition.

[name of your company] has more than XX years of experience in the [name of service] field. We can take your [name of service] worries off your hands. Let us:

- [Name three or four specific advantages your business brings]
- Xxx
- Xxx
- Xxx

See what we've done for [name of previous client]: [testimonial here]

Why not find out for yourself? Call XXX-XXX-XXXX to set up your *free* consultation. If you're one of the first XX callers, you'll also receive a *free* [gift] just for meeting with me.

There is no cost and no obligation. You have nothing to risk!

Get some of your precious time back. Why not call today and take the first step down the road to a less stressful life.

Sincerely,

[your name]

P.S. Call today to receive your *free* [gift]—XXX-XXX-XXXX.

Trash Can Mailer

Caution:

Throwing this letter away may be harmful to your success.

Just in case you're thinking of throwing my letter in the trash, I wanted to help you do it.

Dear [prospective client]:

Are things running smoothly in your business? Or are your operations a little tarnished around the edges? Are you staying ahead of the competition? Or do you find yourself working too hard and not getting the results you want?

If everything is perfect and there's no room for improvement, then **THROW THIS LETTER AWAY . . . YOU DON'T NEED ME.**

But if you'd like to make improvements to your bottom line, then call me!

In just 10 minutes I can show you how to make your business more efficient than ever before. To prove it, I'll give you a *free* Business Review along with a *free* [gift] just for giving up a few minutes of your time.

What's in it for me? Simple. When potential clients learn how much money I can save them in the long run, they see my services as an investment in the future. I make sure that my time and my ideas are of value to today's business owner.

If you're tired of the same results you're currently getting, then you need to do something different!

Just accept my offer for a *free*, no obligation, Business Review. In just 10 minutes I'll show how you can be making at least $1,000 profit starting right now!

I'll show you how to:

- Save money.
- Improve your bottom line profit.
- Reduce stress.
- Improve [name an action].
- [Add your own unique benefit here].

I guarantee my offer. I am so sure that I can instantly show you areas with a minimum value of $1,000 (in savings or money making ideas) that I'll pay YOU if you believe that my review wasn't worth at least $1,000. Yes, I'll pay the charity of your choice $25 in cash. You can't lose!

Call today! You can reach me at XXX-XXX-XXXX to receive your *free* Business Review and [gift].

Sincerely,

[Your Name, Company Name]

Warning Mailer

WARNING:

Do Your Restaurants Make These Critical Mistakes?

The difference between average and exceptional is in the details. When you're looking for excellence in a restaurant, you need to know some small secrets about the industry that can make all the difference in your experience. Here's a list of things that most restaurants hope you'll never find out.

Reheating: Your meal was probably made this morning and has been heated and reheated throughout the day. This means it doesn't have the fresh-from-the-oven taste. Ask your server when your meal was prepared.

Concentrate: Fresh should mean fresh. Many restaurants say they use fresh ingredients but actually used canned and prepackaged substitutes to save time and money. Which would you rather have?

No VIP Program: As a loyal customer, you deserve more. Many restaurants don't offer they regular customers anything extra. Ask what benefits you receive as a repeat customer.

It's All in the Details: Look for signs of customer care and attention to detail. Is the staff polite? Do they call you by name? Look at the atmosphere. Is the restaurant clean? Are the staff's uniforms impeccable? A superior restaurant takes great pride in the details.

Come in and see how Joe's Restaurant shows you we care about your business.

Joe's Restaurants
123 Any Street
My Town, State, Zip
555-123-4567
Sunday through Thursday 6:00 AM to 11:00 PM.
Friday and Saturday 6:00 AM to midnight
VISA, MasterCard, American Express, Discover

Newsletter Article Promotion

One marketing tool that very effectively accomplishes all the desired actions is the newspaper front-page article. It is a mock newspaper

THE BUSINESS CHRONICLE

March 2007   Weather: Excellent for increasing business   Phone: (480) 969-1738   Free for smart business owners

Mitch Carson named 'Outstanding Entrepreneur Of The Year'

Shareholders thrilled, competitors stunned as company profits double in less than 12 months

Special Report by Travis Lawrence.

Chatsworth, CA - Mitch Carson and Impact Products have just realized the most successful six months ever.

"I can't believe what's happened to our business," said Mitch Carson of Impact Products. "If you asked me six months ago whether or not we could double our sales while slashing our costs in half I would not have believed it possible. However, six months ago I decided to get really serious about improving our business. I realized that if we wanted to become the dominant player in our market that we were going to have to do a lot of things differently.

"I was sick and tired of competitors undercutting our margins, ads and marketing campaigns that weren't pulling the results we needed, sales people who were barely making enough sales to justify their existence, and a high turnover of customers.

"I responded to an offer for a free marketing consultation from business development consultant, Martin Howey, who promised that in little more than an than an hour, he could show me how to generate a minimum of $5,000 in newfound profits in the next 30 days, using ideas that I could implement for very little time, money, effort, or risk.

"Martin, is a TopLine Business Solutions associate, who's successes include companies such

as, AT&T, Pet Foods, Black & Decker, General Mills, Ralston Purina, Pacific Power & Light, Blue Cross-Blue Shield, Deluxe Check Imprinters, Coca Cola USA, Hewlett Packard, IDS/American Express, and a host of other businesses, convinced me that he knows his stuff.

"I can now see why the top companies are so successful and how they stay there. The ideas Martin shared with me were simple, step-by-step and virtually turnkey.

"The amazing thing was, Martin didn't try to sell us anything. The consultation was absolutely free... it cost us nothing! But the ideas we picked up made so much sense that we could see that we would be foolish to continue in business without Martin's continued help and coaching. Now we've enlisted Martin's services on an on-going basis, and have gained the competitive edge we were looking for. And we did it without expensive advertising, discounting our prices or having to work any harder.

"I could not have done it without the help of Martin Howey," Mitch continued. "Some of the areas we discussed included; Low-cost or no-cost ways to get more new customers, how to increase our prospect-to-customer conversion rate, how to increase the average dollar amount of every sale, how to get our customers to buy from us more often and do business with us for a longer period of time, how to effectively increase our margins, how to build a referral-based business, and much more.

"As a result we now completely dominate our marketplace," exuded Mitch. "We thought it was important to involve our staff in this process. They

President George W. Bush congratulates Mitch Carson's efforts – nominates Mitch for 'National Entrepreneur Of The Year.'

not only loved being included, but our staff turnover has diminished by 85%!".

According to sources close to the company, the success of Mitch Carson's marketing initiative even reached the President's office. Mr Bush's comment was, "If all businesses have the vision and marketing savvy of Mitch Carson, the nation's industry will continue to thrive and excel. I congratulate Mitch on such outstanding vision and initiative!" said Mr. Bush.

Of course, the best thing about Mitch Carson's healthy profit increase is that the business is more fun and Mitch has far more time for family and other interests.

According to our confidential sources at the National Business Bureau, Mitch Carson's retirement as a philanthropic millionaire and community leader are mere formalities now. In fact, reports have it that Mitch has been sited vacationing in St. Tropez and other exclusive global hideaways with family and friends, enjoying a well-earned break.

In Mitch's parting words, "If you are serious about freeing yourself from your business, then you must take up Martin's FREE offer!"

If you want to make this a reality, you can contact Martin Howey at (480) 969-1738.

---

article that is customized with a specific prospect's name and addresses the major concerns that they are facing and offers solutions to correct or eliminate those concerns.

The article is printed on a letter-size sheet, placed in a frame and sent to specific and targeted prospects via courier, UPS, FedEx, USPS Priority Mail, or other such services. When it arrives at the prospect's business, its large size and priority delivery packaging immediately attracts attention, evokes importance, bypasses the receptionist or secretary (gatekeeper), lands on the desk of the intended recipient, and compels them to open it on the spot.

That's the first step. Getting to the right person, getting noticed, and getting opened.

When the package is opened, the recipient immediately sees a framed article with the heading of a newspaper, the name of their business in a bold and interest-generating headline, and a picture of the president.

The article tells a story from the business owner's perspective about how he was facing some problems in his business such as:

- Being sick and tired of competitors undercutting his margins,
- Ads and marketing campaigns that weren't pulling the results they needed,
- Salespeople who were barely making enough sales to justify their existence, or
- A high turnover of customers.

He goes on to tell about how he responded to an offer from a business development consultant who made an offer of a free consultation and promised some impressive and compelling benefits. The consultant's credentials established him as an authority and the free consultation provided enough good ideas that the business owner admitted that he would be foolish to not use the consultant.

He then tells how they discussed:

- How to use low-cost or no-cost ways to get more new customers,
- How to increase their prospect-to-customer conversion rate,
- How to increase the average dollar amount of every sale,
- How to get their customers to buy from them more often and do business with them for a longer period of time,
- How to effectively increase their margins,
- How to build a referral-based business, and much more.

These are things every business owner would like to know how to do. Then he talks about the results he's achieved:

- They completely dominate their marketplace.
- They involved their staff in the process.
- Their staff love being a apart of it.
- Their staff turnover diminished by 85 percent.

Next came a commendation by the president, followed by the business owner having:

- A healthy profit increase,
- More fun in the business,
- Far more time for family and other interests,
- Retirement as a philanthropic millionaire and community leader, or even
- A vacation in an exotic location.

Finally, an endorsement by the business owner of the consultant's services followed by a call to action.

Of course, the letter is fictitious. It's not true. A cover letter points that out and explains that if the business owner can relate to the concerns itemized in the article and if they would like to eliminate those concerns and have the benefits that the article described, that there is a good possibility that by working together the consultant and owner could achieve them. The letter then asks for an appointment to discuss in detail how those benefits could indeed become a reality.

If after three or four days the business owner hasn't contacted the consultant, a follow-up telephone call is in order. The consultant simply calls the prospect and asks if he received the framed article and, if so, does he have it hanging on his wall yet?

In most cases, that will provoke a laugh from the prospect, the ice is broken and he will mention how creative the idea was, and getting an appointment is a mere formality.

This is one of the most effective and results-producing marketing tools some of the top marketing and business development consultants use to get appointments with some very high-level and influential prospects. It is not a mass-mailing piece. It is designed to target very specific people in a very creative way to catch their attention, hit some of their hot buttons, and get them to want to know more about the offer.

X-Ray Mailer

This is one of our most effective mailers. It can be used as a one-time mailer or as an introduction for a series of mailers. The primary strategy of the X-ray mailer is an introduction or a reminder of a service, product,

idea, business, or person. Most people do not like to read sales letters because they are the same as any other boring junk mail they receive. But the X-ray is a proven strategy that will draw in the prospect to read what is on the letter, just as you are probably doing right this moment. But if you do have more to say, the X-ray can be the eye catcher to cause the prospect to read the attached sales letter. We can even stick on a note with messages, such as "Please hold up to the light to see your prescription," to boost the consumer to read the message on the X-ray. Ultimately, it is a fun and enjoyable method for the prospect to consume your message. Another plus: postage is generally inexpensive for this mailer. Most other mailers have costly postage because of their bulk and weight, but the X-ray mailer is flat and lightweight.

Examples, Ideas, and Concepts

- Financial institutions can use this mailer to tell their customer to have an X-ray of their money going to waste. This will send a message to use their services to manage their money the right way.

- Automobile repair companies can send these mailers out as a reminder for their clients to get an X-ray (maintenance, oil change, tune-up, etc.) of their car.

Sweet Mailer Programs

Pearls: Can be used for giveaways, particularly on Mother's Day and on Valentine's Day.

For example, a seafood restaurant could advertise free pearls for a meal purchase on Valentine's Day. Mother's Day can be stretched to be "Mom's Month."

Bottle Mailers: Can be used as advertising mailers. The bottle is an attention grabber.

For example, an automotive company can use the slogan: "Don't be stranded without your keys/map."

For example, you might use the slogan: "Find buried treasure right in your own company!"

Bank Bags with Secure Tape: Used primarily for unique mailers, it's most effective when coupled with a CD to complement the sales letter.

For example, you might use the slogan: "You'll need this bag to hold all your money while running to the bank!"

For example, you might use the slogan: "You can trust us to handle your finances."

Silver Platter and Red Eagle 9 × 2 Envelope: Used for multi-step mailings.

For example Slogan: "You are our top priority and we will make sure to serve you on a silver platter."

Trash Can w/Crumpled Letter: Can be used for mailings.

For example, you might use the slogan: "Don't throw away this incredible one time opportunity!"

For example, you might use the slogan: "Don't throw your commissions away!"

For example, you might use the slogan: "Previous attempts have ended up in the trash, so I saved you the time today."

Million-Dollar Bills: Can be used as stuffers with sales letters for mailings.

For example, you might use the slogan: "We'll make you a million bucks!"

For example, you might use the slogan: "MILLION-DOLLAR opportunities like this one don't come by very often . . ."

Shredded Money: Can be used for mailings.

For example, a finance company might use the slogan: "Without my help, your money could end up like this."

For example, you might use the slogan: "Our rates tear up the competition!"

Worry Dolls: Can be used as a stuffer for bottle mailer. Worry dolls have a story to tell and can tie into many promotions. The children of Guatemala place these dolls under their pillows at night and believe their worries will go away by morning.

For example, an investment company might use the slogan: "Don't worry. We can solve all your financial problems!"

Vacation Vouchers: Can be used as a high-end giveaway for just visiting your store or making an appointment for a consultation.

Needle in a Haystack: Used for mailings to separate your business/company from the competition.

> For example, you might use the slogan: "Tired of needling through the competition? Let us bale you out!"

> For example, you might use the slogan: "Finding the right (your profession) is like searching for a needle in a haystack."

Tuits: Can be used as stuffers with sales letters. They are lightweight, use little postage, and the bulkiness will cause consumers to open your letters.

> For example, you might use the slogan: "Make sure you can get a Round *Tuit!*"

> For example, you might use the slogan: "Bring in this token for a free consultation."

Coconuts with Mini Pack of Sunscreen: Can be used for mailings. One of the best attention grabbers. May be used for a beach theme.

> For example, can be used in the beginning of summer for mailings to offer summer promotions.

> For example, can also be used for invitations; can be a unique momentum booster for a special occasion.

Boomerangs: Can be used for mailings to reactivate clients.

> For example, you might use the slogan: "We want you back!"

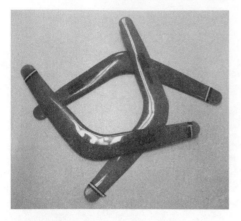

Crayon 4-Pack: Can be used for mailers with child-like sales letter.

Scratch-Offs: Can be used for mailings. Also, can be used for a preshow promotion that can excite potential customers before the show begins

For example, offer prizes to those who answer questions correctly.

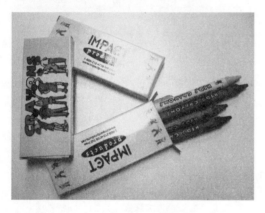

Frisbees: Can be used for mailers. It includes an insert for your sales letter or any other item in back of the Frisbee. Can be used for a beach or park theme.

For example, use in the beginning of spring to offer promotions.

For example, you might use the slogan: "Toss us your idea. . . . We'll toss back results!"

Sample Carpet Cleaning Promotion

Second Notice!
Your Free Offer
Expires Soon!

"You and your family are inhaling dirt, filth and grime every day!"

Dear <First Name>,

As you can see, I've enclosed a packet of dirt with this letter. Why? Actually, there are a couple of reasons:

1. To show you what you and your family are inhaling every day in your home!
2. I'd like to show you how I can save you thousands of dollars in carpet cleaning, carpet replacement and medical care.

Your carpet can hold 8 times its weight in toxin—filled dirt!

Moving is Hectic!

We understand that moving can be enormously hectic. In fact, getting your carpets and furniture cleaned may be one of the last things on your to-do list. But experts agree that regular carpet cleaning can improve the health of your family and extend the life of your carpet. Isn't it important that you start your family out in your new home with the cleanest environment possible?

But how do you find a carpet cleaner you can trust in a new town? You ask around, right? Well, more than (client base number) of your neighbors already know why our company is the ideal solution for your family's carpet and furniture cleaning needs.

Your family deserves a healthy home!

A Personal Invitation

So to help you discover what your neighbors already know, I'd like to invite you and your entire family for a **complete Carpet Audit™ of your carpet's health and longevity—all at no cost to you!** And as a special welcome to the neighborhood, I'll give you a **free genuine freshwater pearl necklace ($____value).** The total value of this complimentary welcome package is $_____!

Save Money!

If you're like me, you may be skeptical about any company that offers a discount on its services. I don't blame you! But I understand that moving is expensive and now, more than ever, saving money is important to your family.

I'm also confident that you meet our professional inspectors and technicians and experience our five-star service, you won't want to go anywhere else for your family's carpet and furniture care.

So please take a few minutes to read this letter and discover how **you and your family can save thousands in unnecessary carpet cleaning, replacement and medical costs.**

According to the EPA, an unhealthy carpet can worsen or cause:

- *Infectious disease*
- *Asthma*
- *Rhinitis*
- *Conjunctival inflammation*
- *Recurrent fever*
- *Malaise*
- *Dyspnea*
- *Chest tightness*
- *Cough*

LOGO

Street Address
Address 2
City, ST Zip Code

PHONE   (555) 555-0
FAX   (555) 555-0125
E-MAIL   someone@example.com
WEB SITE http://www.samplesite.com

5 Reasons Why You'll Love Our Services

1. **Our Five-Star Service Guarantee:** Your neighbors love our service because we are committed to perfection. We promise to always:
   - Answer your call anytime, day or night, at (555) 555-0215
   - Schedule an appointment within 24 hours after receiving your call
   - Be on time
   - Do the job right the first time, or do it over without any additional fee
   - Demonstrate our care for your family through our professional appearance and manner and by the products and procedures we use.

2. **Ethical Business Practices:** Too many service providers trick you into expensive treatments. Here's how it goes. They bait you with promotions for services at unbelievably low prices. When they arrive at your home to perform the service, they ding you with additional charges for every spot, over-priced carpet protector, and even pressure you to buy more service than you need! We provide you with a complete estimate upfront—no hidden charges—guaranteed!

3. **The Safest Methods for Your Family:** We have the equipment and expertise to effectively remove dirt and the cleaning liquids used to clean carpets. We know that improper cleaning procedures can void your carpet warranty and shorten the life of your carpet, so rest assured our methods are the safest available. Why take a chance with home or rental equipment that can leave the carpet too wet – promoting mold and fungal buildup – or that leaves detergent behind? Instead, enjoy beautiful results and avoid the headaches of potentially dangerous approaches.

4. **Our Exclusive 11-Step Success Process:** We provide the most comprehensive service available to give you and your family cleanliness you can trust! Here's our formula for success:
   - Inspect your carpet to ensure the best cleaning method and results.
   - Provide a complete estimate—no surprises!
   - Pre-treat spots and stains as necessary.
   - Pre-apply carpet cleaning solution to loosen soil in the carpet.
   - Rinse and extract with clear water to ensure that the cleaning solution and soil are removed along with the rinse water, leaving a clean, residue- and mold-free carpet.
   - Re-treat spots and stains if necessary.
   - Rake carpet after cleaning to align fibers for even appearance.
   - Apply carpet protector (upon request).
   - Move and replace furniture in its original position.
   - Protect carpet from furniture during the drying process.
   - Make sure you are happy with the finished product!

5. **No-Risk, Money Back Guarantee:** If for any reason you are unsatisfied with your service, we'll either make you happy or you won't pay—it's that simple! We can say we do this only because we are so confident you will absolutely love our services.

LOGO	Street Address Address 2 City, ST Zip Code	PHONE (555) 555-0125 FAX (555) 555-0125 E-MAIL someone@example.com WEB SITE http://www.samplesite.com

It's So Easy to Get Started

Here's how you can take advantage of our introductory offer. Give our friendly staff a call at (555) 555-0215 to set up an appointment for your **free Carpet Audit™ of your carpet's health and longevity**. During this visit, we'll perform a complete inspection of your carpet, including an investigation of potential mold and other health hazards. And before we leave, our expert technician will go over any problem areas and talk about our recommendations for your carpet's care as well as the options that are available to you. All this will take about 60 minutes. And, of course, we'll present you with your **free genuine freshwater pearls**—just for letting us talk with you.

No Selling! No Pressure!

Our goal is to give you the greatest carpet-cleaning experience you've ever had! And if we are pushy or didn't actually care about you and your family, you wouldn't be happy with our service. That's why my staff takes great care to talk with each client personally, educating you about your options so you can make the decision that is right for you and your family.

To schedule your Free Carpet Audit™, call us at (555) 555-0215 today!

But please hurry! To maintain the personalized nature of our practice, we accept only a limited number of new clients each year. Therefore, if you are not one of the first 25 people to call and mention this letter, we will have to give this extraordinary gift to someone else.

You're just a phone call away from the healthy home you've always dreamed of!
Call us at (555) 555-0215 today!

Sincerely,

(Owner's name)

P.S. If you can't take advantage of this offer, please tell a friend. If they mention your name, I'll gladly extend this extraordinary offer to them on your behalf!

LOGO	Street Address Address 2 City, ST Zip Code	PHONE (555) 555-0125 FAX (555) 555-0125 E-MAIL someone@example.com WEB SITE http://www.samplesite.com

Sample Dentist Program

You'll Want to Read This! Finally, Gentle Dentistry with Proven Results!

Welcome to <city>!

Dear <First Name>,

As you can see, I've enclosed a million dollar bill with this letter. Why? Actually, there are a few reasons:

1. You and your family deserve million-dollar smiles and I'd like to help you discover the ideal dental care you deserve.
2. I'd like to show you how I can save you thousands of dollars in unnecessary dental care.
3. Our office can help you keep your teeth healthy and beautiful—for a lifetime!

Moving is Hectic!

We understand that moving can be extremely hectic. In fact, **choosing a dentist may be one of the last things on your to-do list.** But experts agree that visiting a dentist regularly can help prevent tooth decay and other serious disorders that can lead to costly treatment. Did you know that **four out of every five Americans suffers from gum disease**? So you can see why it's important that you and your family stay on track with regular dental exams.

But how do you find a dentist in a new town? You ask around, right? Well, more than (client base number) of your neighbors already know why our office is the ideal solution for your entire family's dental care.

Insert Testimonial Here

Your family deserves million-dollar smiles!

A Personal Invitation

So to help you discover what your neighbors already know, I'd like to invite you and your entire family for a **complete dental examination and cosmetic evaluation—all at no cost to you!** And as a special welcome to the neighborhood, I'll give you and your family **$100 off each whitening procedure**. The total value of this complimentary welcome package is $_____ for each member of your family!

Million-Dollar Smiles!

If you're like me, you may be skeptical about any medical professional who offers a discount on their services. I don't blame you! But I understand that moving is expensive and now, more than ever, saving money is important to your family.

I'm also confident that once you visit our state-of-the-art office, meet our friendly and expert staff and experience our five-star service, you won't want to go anywhere else for your family's dental care.

So please take a few minutes to read this letter and discover how **you and your family can save thousands in unnecessary dental care** by letting us help you take care of your teeth today!

About our Office

At the center of my practice is my heartfelt desire to help you keep your family's teeth healthy and beautiful with as little pain and anxiety as possible. In fact, most of our patients tell us they don't feel a thing! And every member of my staff shares my same desire to make your dental care a pleasure.

Street Address
Address 2
City, ST Zip Code

PHONE　(555) 555-0125
FAX　　(555) 555-0125
E-MAIL　someone@example.com
WEB SITE http://www.samplesite.com

12 Reasons Why You'll Love Our Office

1. **Practically Pain Free Dental Care:** One of the main reasons people love our office is because we do EVERYTHING possible to make sure you don't feel a thing! One of my goals is to make pain, fear and anxiety at the dentist's office **a thing of the past!** And we use the latest technology to make sure that every procedure is as pain-free as possible!

2. **Guilt-Free Office:** Studies show that the number-one reason people put off their dental care has nothing to do with fear or pain, but rather with the guilt of having putting off the dentist. No lectures and no worries—we'll get your dental care right back on track!

3. **Affordable Care for the Entire Family:** We know that dental care can sometimes present unexpected costs. And if you're one of the 108 million Americans without dental insurance, we have payment options that can make your dental care even more comfortable—we'll even let you extend payments for as long as 48 months! And if you do have insurance, we gladly accept most major plans.

4. **Cavity-Free Kids:** We specialize in helping parents raise cavity-free children. The U.S. Surgeon General cites tooth decay as the single-most chronic childhood disease. But now with improved technology, we can help eliminate tooth decay in your kids! The bottom line? Your kid is healthier and more confident and you save money!

5. **Straight Teeth for Teens:** There is nothing more important than setting your teenagers' teeth straight before it gets too late. And we offer the hottest trends in stylish mouthgear to keep you teenager happy!

6. **Invisalign:** We offer the newest technology is teeth-straightening—invisible and comfortable—for children and adults!

7. **State-of-the-Art Cerec 3D Equipment:** No more temporary crowns, gooey impressions or second cementation appointments! We can make your crown or inlay right in our office in about an hour.

8. **Music and Movies:** Enjoy your favorite tunes and flicks during your exams and treatment.

9. **No Waiting Room:** When you come to our office, you'll notice that you don't wait a second. The moment you show up, your care begins. And if you ever wait longer than 15 minutes, we'll knock $25 off your bill.

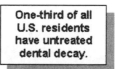

One-third of all U.S. residents have untreated dental decay.

10. **Instant Emergency Service:** If you ever experience a dental emergency, I'll make sure you are seen immediately! Your dental health is my number-one priority!

11. **No-Risk, Money Back Guarantee:** If for any reason you are unsatisfied with your care, we'll either make you happy or you won't pay—it's that simple! We can say we do this only because we are so confident you will absolutely love your visit.

12. **Free Tour and Toothbrushes:** And when you come by for your complimentary appointment, we'll give you a complete tour of our office and free toothbrushes for everyone in your home!

Street Address
Address 2
City, ST Zip Code

PHONE   (555) 555-0125
FAX   (555) 555-0125
E-MAIL   someone@example.com
WEB SITE http://www.samplesite.com

It's So Easy to Get Started

Here's how you can take advantage of our introductory offer. Give our friendly staff a call at (office telephone number) to set up an appointment for your **free dental examination and cosmetic evaluation**. Be sure to ask for (name) and tell her you received a special New Resident Invitation. During your visit, we'll perform a complete dental exam, including cancer screening and x-rays, for every member of your family. And before you leave, I'll go over any problem areas and show you actual photographs of your teeth with our new intra-oral camera. We'll also talk about my recommendations for your care and all the options that are available to you. All this will take about 60 minutes.

Dentistry the Way it Should Be

Our goal is to give you the best dental experience you've ever had! That's why my staff takes great care to talk with each client personally, educating you about your options so you can make the decision that is right for you and your family.

Insert
Testimonial
Here

To schedule your Free Million-Dollar Smile Consultation, call us at (office phone number) today!

But please hurry! To maintain the personalized nature of our practice, we accept only a limited number of new clients each month. **Be one of the first 25 people to call** and mention this letter, and get this extraordinary gift offer for you and your family!

You're just a phone call away from the smile you've always dreamed of! Call us now at (office phone number) today!

Sincerely,

(Dentist Name), DDS

P.S. If you can't take advantage of this offer, please tell a friend. If they mention your name, I'll gladly extend this extraordinary offer to them on your behalf!

P.P.S. If you're unsure or have any questions, please don't hesitate to call one of our friendly and experienced dental health counselors today!

Insert
Testimonial
Here

Street Address Address 2 City, ST Zip Code	PHONE (555) 555-0125 FAX (555) 555-0125 E-MAIL someone@example.com WEB SITE http://www.samplesite.com

I STILL HAVE A GIFT FOR YOU!

Indicia

Okay, so maybe the last thing on your mind is finding a new dentist. So we'll make it easy for you be extending our offer for a **Free Million-Dollar Smile Consultation** for your entire family! We have just a few spots left for this complete exam and consultation ($_____ value), so call (555) 555-0215 today!

Dentist Name
Address 1
Address 2
City, ST ZIP Code

Your *FREE* Package Includes:

- **Complete oral and dental exam**
- **Oral cancer screening**
- **X-rays**
- **Cosmetic consultation**
- **Personalized recommendations**

RECIPIENT ADDRESS

All for your entire family!

GIFT CERTIFICATE

Presented to: _____ *Your Family* _____

From: _____ *(Dentist Name)* _____

The bearer of this certificate is entitled to:

_____ *Million-Dollar Smile Consultation* _____

(Value $_____)

To schedule your appointment, call (555) 555-0215 today!
Gifts are limited to the first 25 recipients.

Street Address
Address 2
City, ST Zip Code

PHONE (555) 555-0125
FAX   (555) 555-0125
E-MAIL someone@example.com
WEB   www.samplesite.com

LAST CHANCE!
THIS IS YOUR FINAL NOTICE!

Indicia

We haven't heard from you but want you to know that your family's oral health is our number-one priority! That's why we wanted to send you just one more reminder that our offer for a **Free Million-Dollar Smile Consultation** for your entire family is about to expire! We have just a few spots left for this complete exam and consultation ($_____ value), so call (555) 555-0215 today!

Dentist Name
Address 1
Address 2
City, ST ZIP Code

high-res image would expand to fit

Your *FREE* Package Includes:

- Complete oral and dental exam
- Oral cancer screening
- X-rays
- Cosmetic consultation
- Personalized recommendations

RECIPIENT ADDRESS

All for your entire family!

Here's Why You Shouldn't Give Us The Brush-Off!

Is this farewell? Your family's smiles are important to us, but we haven't heard from you about your **Free Million-Dollar Smile Consultation** for your entire family! We understand that life is hectic and have held a spot for your complete exam and consultation ($_____ value).

In just a couple of days, we'll release your spot to those on our waiting list. If you'd still like to take advantage of this amazing offer, call (555) 555-0215 today!

And if that still doesn't tempt you, we'll give you an **additional special gift** during your appointment! So call today and don't lose out!

(DENTIST NAME)'S TOP-FIVE REASONS TO CALL TODAY:

1. Practically Pain Free Dental Care: We do EVERYTHING possible to make sure you don't feel a thing! And music and movies keep you entertained while we work.

2. Affordable Care for the Entire Family: We have payment options that can make your dental care even more comfortable. And if you do have insurance, we gladly accept most major plans.

3. Cavity-Free Kids: We specialize in helping parents raise cavity-free children. The bottom line? Your kid is healthier and more confident and you save money!

4. No-Risk, Money Back Guarantee: If you're not happy, we fix it or it's free!

5. Free Consultation for the Entire Family: See the other side for details!

Sample Realtor Program

Howdy, naybor! My name is Mathew. Will you be my friend?

My daddy Jirius runs an honest real estate bizness and it is right down the street! And I talked him into giving you a free insert offer!

Mommy sez I am trying to buy new friends. What does that mean? Lets meet and play and be friends!

You will ♥ my dad's way of doing bizness. His clients ♥ him! Do you know Mrs. insert name? She says it is tuff to find a great realtor in a city this big. Espeshally one you can count on! Thank goodness for my daddy and Century 21!

Now there is a catch. You gotta make an appoyntment for what. Mommy says daddy runs a pretty tight ship! He will want to come to your to meet you.

So call my daddy Jirius today at insert phone number! I know you will ♥ my dad. Everyone does!

C U later alligator!

Mathew

P.S. I am 7. How old are you?
P.P.S. Enjoy your new crayons!

Espeshally one you can count on! Thank goodness for my daddy and Century 21!

Now there is a catch. You gotta make an appoyntment for what . Mommy says daddy runs a pretty tight ship! He will want to come to your to meet you.

So call my daddy Jirius today at insert phone number ! I know you will♡ my dad. Everyone does! C U later alligator! Mathew

P.S. I am 7. How old are you? P.P.S. Enjoy your new crayons!

Sample UPS Store Program

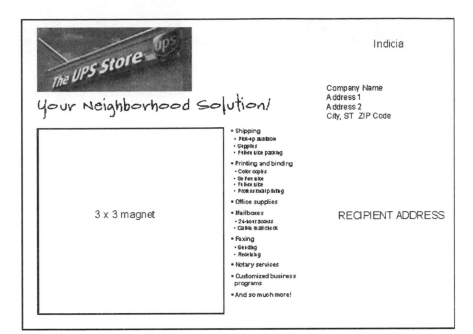

Indicia

Company Name
Address 1
Address 2
City, ST ZIP Code

Your Neighborhood Solution!

- Shipping
  - Pick-up available
  - Supplies
  - Full-service packing
- Printing and binding
  - Color copies
  - Self-service
  - Full-service
  - Professional printing
- Office supplies
- Mailboxes
  - 24-hour access
  - Call-in mail check
- Faxing
  - Sending
  - Receiving
- Notary services
- Customized business programs
- And so much more!

3 x 3 magnet

RECIPIENT ADDRESS

we treat you like family!

Moving Is Hectic!
We know that moving to a new home is a busy time for any family. That's why we want to let you know that we're here to help!

Who Can You Trust?
Helpful people and great services right in your neighborhood—that's what your local UPS Store offers! You'll find all the quality services you've come to expect from a neighborhood shop plus the full capabilities of the UPS network.

Business or Pleasure
Whether you use our services for business or pleasure, you'll still get the same great personalized service! With great shipping options, full-service packaging, mailbox or document services, copying and printing services, you can get it all done at your neighborhood The UPS Store location. And with more than 3,000 locations in the U.S., you'll find our convenient services wherever you go!

| COUPON | COUPON | COUPON |

Sample Insurance Sequential Mailers

BIG INSURANCE COMPANY
123 Main Street
Your Town, ST 12121
555-555-5555
Date
Susan Johnson
456 Elm Avenue
Your Town, ST 12456
Dear Mrs. Johnson:
Welcome to your new home. Now might be a good time to consider reviewing your insurance policies.

This is especially important if you're not already insured with Big Insurance Company. As a Big Insurance Company agent, I can handle all your insurance needs.

In a few days, I'll contact you with a special gift—a Big Insurance Company Road Atlas. You can contact me at 555-5555, or return the attached tear-off reply if you need to reach me before then.

Sincerely,

I'd also like information on:

❏ Auto insurance

❏ Homeowners insurance

❏ Health insurance

❏ Review of my insurance file

❏ Car financing

❏ Other_____

Frank Thompson, CLU, LUTC
President

Yes. . . . I'd like to know more about Big Insurance Company's insurance review.

Please call me at _____

Best time to call _____

Susan Johnson
456 Elm Avenue
Your Town, ST 12456
ATTENTION: Frank Thompson
Big Insurance Company
P.O. Box 555
Midwestern Town, IL 20202

Sequential Letter 1

Hi, Susan . . . as you can see, I've attached a nice, crisp "million dollar bill" to the top of this letter. And, I've done it for three reasons:

1. Because you've just moved into the area, you're now one of my neighbors, and hopefully will become one of my friends. And because good friends are hard to come by, when you find one, they're worth a million.

2. What I have to say is very important to say, and I wanted to catch your attention.

3. Finally, my message has to do with money—a LOT of money—and this "million dollar bill" is representative of a goal that we can achieve by working together.

Most people who live in this area, over their working lifetime, will earn well over a million dollars. The steps you take now, with your insurance coverage can mean the difference between losing it all, protecting it with safety and security, or maximizing and enhancing its value.

One of the biggest challenges people face when moving to a new area, is who to trust to handle their needs. If they make the wrong choice, it could be devastating for them and their family's future security.

(Continued)

If they make the right choice, they can not only be assured of getting the best value for their insurance dollar, but they can rest easily knowing that they are appreciated, well taken care of, and are enjoying a refreshingly fun and enjoyable business relationship.

It's no wonder why so many of your neighbors choose to do business with our agency. If you'd like to know more about why they're so happy with our service, I invite you to contact Sheila, my Office Manager, to arrange a time that we can get together. It typically only takes about 17 minutes.

So, please call Sheila right away. . . . I know you're going to be pleased.

Your Name

P.S . . . I'm so confident that our time will be well spent, and that I can show you some solid reasons to do business with my agency, that I'll bring along a $25.00 blank check. If you don't agree that our meeting provided valuable information to you (regardless of whether or not we end up doing business together), I'll let you fill in the name of your favorite charity, and I'll make the donation in your name.

Your Insurance Agency
Your Name, Agent
123 Main Street, Your Town, State Zip
Voice: 000-000-0000 Fax: 000-000-0000
E-mail: agents name@yourname.com
web site: www.agentsname.com

Sequential Letter 2

Hi, Susan. . . . It's me again. Remember, I'm the one who sent you the "million dollar bill" a few days ago.

My last letter talked about *big* money . . . how to protect your valuable assets from sudden and unexpected loss, and at the same time, benefit from a fun and refreshingly enjoyable business relationship (something that's sorely missing in too many businesses today).

Because I haven't heard from you yet, I thought I'd attach a real **one-dollar bill**, and talk to you for a moment about *real* money . . . the kind of money that inadvertently slips through most people's hands every day.

I'm going to be right up front with you, and let you know that in actuality, there is really very little difference in most insurance policies from one insurance company to another. The real difference (and where most people waste thousands of dollars), is in the types and amounts of coverage they purchase, and the agent and agency they choose to handle their insurance needs.

If you'll take just a minute to give Sheila, my Office Manager, a call, she'll help find a time that's convenient for us to get together so I can show you why so many of your neighbors choose us to help them not only make smart *real* money decisions, but *big* money decisions, as well.

As I mentioned in my last letter, I know your time will be well invested.

Looking forward to seeing you soon,

Your Name

P.S. Remember what I said in my last letter: I'm so confident that our time will be well spent, and that I can show you some solid reasons to do business with my agency, that I'll bring along a $25.00 blank check. If you don't agree that our meeting provided valuable information to you (regardless of whether or not we end up doing business together), I'll let you fill in the name of your favorite charity, and I'll make the donation in your name.

Your Insurance Agency
Your Name, Agent
123 Main Street, Your Town, State Zip
Voice: 000-000-0000 Fax: 000-000-0000
E-mail: agentsname@yourname.com
web site: www.agentsname.com

Sequential Letter 3

Hi, Susan . . .

Yep, it's me again . . . the person who's trying to save you *real big* money by making sure your insurance policies are up to date, that you're not paying for coverage that you don't need, and that you're getting the best value for your insurance dollar possible.

(Continued)

By now, you've no doubt noticed that the amount of money that's attached to the top of each letter is getting smaller. In fact, this letter only has a quarter attached to it.

Know what else is getting smaller with the passage of time? Actually, a couple of things . . .

1. The amount of money you may save by failing to get together with me.
2. The mental peace and security you'll have, not knowing for sure if you're carrying the right coverages on your insurance policies.

Really, it only takes a few minutes for me to look over your policies and give you that all-important second opinion . . . you know, the one that will either confirm that you're okay (in which case, you can rest easy). Or, point out a couple of areas that you may want to consider changing or updating.

Please give Sheila, my Office Manager, a call. She'll be glad to find a time that's convenient for us to get together so I can show how to keep your hard-earned money from slipping through your hands.

As I mentioned in my last letter, I know your time will be well invested.

Looking forward to seeing you soon,

Your Name

P.S. Remember what I said in my last letter: I'm so confident that our time will be well spent, and that I can show you some solid reasons to do business with my agency, that I'll bring along a $25.00 blank check. If you don't agree that our meeting provided valuable information to you (regardless of whether or not we end up doing business together), I'll let you fill in the name of your favorite charity, and I'll make the donation in your name.

Your Insurance Agency
Your Name, Agent
123 Main Street, Your Town, State Zip
Voice: 000-000-0000 Fax: 000-000-0000
E-mail: agentsname@yourname.com
web site: www.agentsname.com

Sequential Letter 4

Susan . . .

Just thought I'd get my two cents in one more time.

Any more, most people won't bother to bend over to pick up a couple of pennies.

I know it doesn't seem like much, but getting two cents worth of advice from someone who's helped so many your neighbors save *real big* money on their insurance, and/or better protect their valuable assets and future earnings from loss, can be one of the most cents-able things you can do.

Let's get together soon. Please give Sheila, my Office Manager, a call. She'll be glad to find a time that's convenient for us to get together so I can show how to keep your hard-earned money from slipping through your hands.

As I mentioned in my last letter, I know your time will be well invested.

Looking forward to seeing you soon,

Your Name

P.S. Remember what I said in my last letter: I'm so confident that our time will be well spent, and that I can show you some solid reasons to do business with my agency, that I'll bring along a $25.00 blank check. If you don't agree that our meeting provided valuable information to you (regardless of whether or not we end up doing business together), I'll let you fill in the name of your favorite charity, and I'll make the donation in your name.

Your Insurance Agency
Your Name, Agent
123 Main Street, Your Town, State Zip
Voice: 000-000-0000 Fax: 000-000-0000
E-mail: agentsname@yourname.com
web site: www.agentsname.com

Sequential Letter 5

Susan . . .

I know what you're thinking . . . "What? No money?!"

Nope. Not this time.

(Continued)

Instead, I'm giving you an apology and a small packet of Tylenol tablets.

Why am I doing this?

Well, the apology is because in my last four letters to you, I've tried my darndest to help you see the value in meeting with me to review your insurance policies . . . but somehow, I haven't succeeded.

The Tylenol tablets are to relieve the stress and giant headache from not knowing for sure if you're properly covered and are getting the best value possible for your insurance dollar.

Of course, there is a better, more permanent way to relieve the stress.

You already know what that is . . .

Just give Sheila, my Office Manager, a call. She'll be glad to find a time that's convenient for us to get together so I can show how to keep your hard-earned money from slipping through your hands.

Believe me, Susan, I wouldn't keep writing to you if I didn't know for sure that your time will be well invested.

The longer you wait, the longer you delay getting the same protection, savings, comfort, and peace of mind so many of your neighbors are getting. So why not pick up the phone and give us a call. . . . I know it will be in your best interest.

Your Name

P.S. Don't forget my promise: I'm so confident that our time will be well spent, and that I can show you some solid reasons to do business with my agency, that I'll bring along a $25.00 blank check. If you don't agree that our meeting provided valuable information to you (regardless of whether or not we end up doing business together), I'll let you fill in the name of your favorite charity, and I'll make the donation in your name.

Your Insurance Agency
Your Name, Agent
123 Main Street, Your Town, State Zip
Voice: 000-000-0000 Fax: 000-000-0000
E-mail: agents name@yourname.com
web site: www.agentsname.com

Holiday Promotions

Special events are cause for celebration. And where better for your customers to celebrate than at your business? We've developed a series of promotions that will keep your company at the forefront of your customer's mind.

From holidays to birthdays and anniversaries, we've ideas for every event. And don't hesitate to make up your own occasion. After all, shouldn't your company celebrate its own anniversary? And shouldn't it have its own holiday? Get creative, have fun, and watch the customers roll in.

Holidays and events are a fun and regular way to drive traffic to your restaurant. By offering a small freemium to diners, our clients have increased their business by as much as 30 percent in one month. What could you do with 30 percent more income?

We've developed more than 20 holiday templates for you to customize and use with your clientele. Just add your logo, address information, and any other details you'd like to include and you're all set.

Direct Mail

Send regular mailings to your database about ongoing holiday promotions. Send them often enough and your customers will start to look for your envelope in their mailbox—just to see what you've come up with next. Be sure to time your mailings so that they'll have enough time to plan to come in but not enough time to forget about your special event. Of course, major holidays require additional planning time both for your customer and your facility.

In-House Promotion

Promote events to your regular customers with countertop signs, posters, and table tents. You'll keep them coming back week after week to join your fun and innovative celebrations. Promote events as many as three weeks in advance to keep the anticipation level high.

Here's a list of holidays and celebrations we've uncovered that you can commemorate every year. Some are familiar, others just a little crazy. Dates may vary so check a current calendar. You may also find fun information on the Web. One site we like is www.holiday.net or www.about.com.

January
New Year's Day
Three Kings Day (Dia de los Santos Reyes)
Martin Luther King Jr. Day
Academy Awards
Trivia Day
Elvis Presley Day
International Thank You Day
Super Bowl Sunday

February
Chinese New Near
Groundhog Day
Lincoln's Birthday
Valentine's Day
President's Day
Washington's Birthday
Mardi Gras
Fat Tuesday
Leap Year
Black History Month

March
Mardi Gras
Fat Tuesday
Ash Wednesday
First Day of Spring
Islamic New Year
Purim
St. Patrick's Day
National Noodle Month
National Peanut Month
National Hot Day

April
April Fool's Day
Passover
Good Friday
Easter
Earth Day
Shakespeare's Birthday
Arbor Day
National Frog Month

May
May Day
Cinco de Mayo
Mother's Day
Memorial Day
Teacher Appreciation Week
Graduation Month

June
Flag Day
Father's Day
Children's Day
Juneteenth
First Day of Summer
Graduation Month

July
Independence Day
National Ice Cream Month

August
Hottest Month of the Year
National Smile Week
National Golf Month

September
Labor Day
Grandparents Day
Rosh Hashanah
Back to School
National Chicken Month
Child Safety Week
National Hispanic Heritage Month
First Day of Fall
Johnny Appleseed Day

October
Yom Kippur
Columbus Day
Boss' Day
Sweetest Day
Halloween
Statue of Liberty's Birthday
World Food Day

November
All Saint's Day
All Soul's Day
Election Day
Veterans Day
Thanksgiving

December
Winter Solstice
First Day of Winter
Hanukkah
Christmas
Kwanzaa
Boxing Day

New Year's Eve
National Pie Day
National Cookie Day
Walt Disney's Birthday

Gemstone Promotions

Everyone loves jewelry. And with more and more competition in the gemstone industry every day, prices are more affordable than ever. And that means that you can offer your customers the glamour of jewelry and gemstones at prices you just won't believe.

Birthday Promotions

Celebrate your customers' birthdays with their birthstone. Semi-precious and simulated stones set in elegant jewelry is a gift they won't soon forget. Here's a list of the birthstones by month and a short overview of the stone and its symbolism:

January: Garnet

Although often thought of as a reddish gem, garnet can actually range from colorless to black. It symbolizes consistency, perseverance, and good health and is also a power stone. According to legend, it guides its wearer when traveling at night. The stone also supposedly protects the wearer from nightmares and depression. Garnet is the anniversary stone for the second and sixth years of marriage.

February: Amethyst

A fairly common purple to lilac gemstone, amethyst can be fairly opaque or nearly transparent, depending on the stone's quality. It is a member of the quartz family and the most valuable in its group. Amethyst is sensitive to light and can change color if left in the sun. It symbolizes sincerity, security, and peace of mind and, according to legend, drinking from an amethyst chalice will prevent intoxication. Amethyst is the anniversary stone for the fourth, sixth, and seventeenth years of marriage.

March: Aquamarine

A light- to dark-blue gem, aquamarine gets its color from iron. Aquamarine means "sea water" in Latin. It fades if left out in the sun, although it is routinely heat-treated to drive out any green in its coloration. The stone of love and mercy, aquamarine is supposed to ease depression and grief. It symbolizes beauty, honesty, loyalty, love and affection. According to legend, it signifies the awakening of friendship among informal acquaintances and the rejuvenation of long marital relationships. It is also said to have strong protective qualities, especially when immersed in water. Aquamarine is the anniversary gemstone for the sixteenth and nineteenth years of marriage.

April: Diamond

Probably the most famous gemstone, diamonds are usually clear and are the hardest stones found in nature. One of the purest forms of carbon, the diamond also conducts heat better than any other mineral. They are a symbol of love and endurance as well as fearlessness and invincibility. They are said to increase one's clarity of thought. The diamond is the anniversary gemstone for the thirtieth and sixtieth years of marriage as well as the anniversary gift for the tenth year.

May: Emerald

A light- to dark-green gemstone, the emerald gets its color from the elements chromium and vanadium. Emeralds of a deeper green are generally more valued and they are often oiled to improve their apparent clarity and to soften the appearance of any imperfection. Emeralds are said to strengthen memory, quicken intelligence, and assist in predicting the future. They may also aid in physical and emotional healing. The emerald is the anniversary gemstone for the twentieth, thirtieth, and fiftieth years of marriage.

June: Pearl

Not truly a gemstone, pearls are actually formed in shellfish as a reaction to irritants like sand. Cultured pearls may be formed by artificially placing irritants inside mussels. Pearls are generally white, brown, silver, cream, black or pink, depending on the type of shellfish that created them and on the type of water in which the source shellfish lived. Pearls are said to enable introspection and boost self-confidence as well as symbolizing love, modesty, chastity, purity, success and happiness. The freshwater pearl is the anniversary stone for the first year of marriage and the natural pearl is the anniversary stone for the third, twelfth, and thirtieth years of marriage.

July: Ruby

The ruby gets its red color from deposits of chromium and iron. Rubies have consistently been the most valued gem in history and symbolize love and reconciliation as well as passion and promise. According to legend, rubies are also thought to ward away misfortune and illness and are also symbols of success, devotion, and integrity. The ruby is the anniversary stone for the fifteenth and fortieth years of marriage.

August: Peridot

A lime- to olive-green gemstone, peridot is created from volcanic eruptions and is sometimes even found on meteors that have fallen to earth. Peridot symbolizes fame, dignity, and protection and is used to transform dreams into reality. It may also protect wearers from nightmares and evil. Peridot is the anniversary gemstone for the sixteenth year of marriage.

September: Sapphire

Generally thought of as a blue gemstone, sapphires in fact come in every color except for red. The highest quality sapphires have an intense blue shade, holding their color in all angles of light. Sapphires represent truth, sincerity, and consistency as well as commitment and loyalty. According to legend, a sapphire attracts divine favor and protects its wearer from the evils of envy, warding off evil spirits, devils, poisons, sorcery, and ulcers. Sapphires are the anniversary gemstone for the fifth and fortieth years of marriage.

October: Opal

Opals reflect light in many different colors. Generally white, orange, or black, all opals have flecks of purple, red, green, and yellow. Black opals with extremely dark body color have the most brilliant flashes of color and are the most valuable. Transparent opals are the next most valuable, as many layers of color may be seen inside their depths. Opals symbolize hope, happiness, and truth. Black opal is regarded as an extremely lucky stone. The opal is the anniversary gemstone for the fourteenth and eighteenth years of marriage.

November: Topaz

Generally light blue, the topaz may also be found in blue, yellow, pink, brown, green, or clear. It symbolizes strength and good will. Topaz is the anniversary gemstone for the fourth and nineteenth years of marriage. Imperial topaz is the anniversary gemstone for the twenty-third year.

December: Turquoise

Turquoise is a vibrant light blue to green gemstone often coated with a layer of acrylic resin to enhance its color, texture, and hardness. Turquoise supposedly helps one avoid procrastination and it has been thought to warn its wearer of danger or illness by changing color. Turquoise is the anniversary gemstone of the fifth year of marriage.

Anniversary Promotions

Celebrate anniversaries (yours or your customer's) with gemstones for the loving couple. Here's a list of anniversary gemstones:

1st	Freshwater Pearl
2nd	Garnet
3rd	Natural Pearl
4th	Topaz
5th	Sapphire
6th	Garnet, Amethyst
7th	Lapis Lazuli
8th	Aventurine
9th	Tiger-Eye, Lapis Lazuli
10th	Diamond
11th	Hematite, Turquoise
12th	Natural Pearl
13th	Malachite
14th	Opal

15th	Ruby
16th	Peridot, Aquamarine
17th	Citrine, Amethyst
18th	Opal
19th	Aquamarine, Topaz
20th	Emerald
21st	Iolite
22nd	Spinel
23rd	Imperial Topaz
24th	Tanzanite
25th	Sterling Silver
30th	Diamond, Natural Pearl
35th	Emerald, Coral
40th	Ruby
45th	Sapphire
50th	Gold
55th	Emerald, Alexandrite
60th	Diamond
65th	Star Sapphire
75th	Diamond

Success Stories

Fax #1 (with Lee Milteer's endorsement): 22 percent response rate

Mailing #1 (mailing tube with tea stained and torn treasure map): 4 percent response rate

Mailing #2 (treasure chest with dried leaves, gold coins and special offer): 8.5 percent response rate

Follow-up phone call: 4 percent response rate

Follow-up e-mail: 8.5 percent response rate

Cost of materials: $146.95

Cost of time: $2,400.00

Total: $2,546.95

Total profits: $123,000

GLOSSARY OF USEFUL TERMS

The following terms have been gathered during our experience as direct-marketing and promotions consultants. It can seem as though printers, apparel manufacturers, and other vendors speak an entirely different language—and they do! We hope the following information helps you "talk the talk" when speaking with your vendors.

1×1 rib: Also known as 2×2 rib knit trim. The width of each rib is the same as the width between each rib. Helps garment retain elasticity.

2-way zipper: A zipper with two pulls that can be zipped or unzipped from either direction.

All-weather microfiber: 100 percent polyester microfiber with waterproof coating and fully taped seams. Waterproof.

Artwork: The blueprint for an imprint or printing job. Artwork can either be camera-ready (on paper) or digital (computer-file based).

Autotrace: A computer process for scanning artwork and converting it to usable and modifiable formats. Works best for recreating nontext objects with irregular shapes. The most popular Autotrace software is Adobe Streamline.

Bitmap: A type of graphic composed of pixels in a grid. Each pixel or "bit" contains color information for the image. Bitmap graphics formats have a fixed resolution. Resizing a bitmap graphic can result in distortion and jagged edges.

Bleed: Ink printed over the edge of the product, eliminating any visible borders. Edges are usually trimmed to create this effect.

Brushed cotton: Cotton fabric that is brushed to remove excess lint and fibers from the fabric, leaving an ultrasoft, smooth finish.

Camera-ready art: Sharp, clear, black-and-white line artwork rendered on glossy photographic papers. Production-ready.

Chambray: A light denim-like fabric with white threads woven across colored threads.

Clip art: Line drawings, screened pictures, and illustrations created for use in electronic or manual design applications. Royalty-free use.

Color separation: Artwork for a multicolor imprint that has been separated into the four basic colors—cyan (blue), magenta, yellow, and black (CMYK). Each color is applied separately.

Combed cotton: Cotton yarn that has been combed to remove short fibers and straighten or arrange longer fibers for increased breathability. Features a soft band for better comfort.

Cool mesh: Similar to pique knit but with a more open texture for increased breathability. Slightly larger weave than cool mesh and with a denser feel.

Copy: In printing, text used in advertisements or graphic design.

Direct-mail advertising: Advertising matter mailed directly to a customer or prospect.

Direct to plate: A printing technology whereby a computerized imprint is output directly to plate material. Can reduce the cost of printing by eliminating the need for film.

Distributor: An organization that specializes in servicing the promotional needs of end users. While end users generally have ideas for products and services needed, distributors have the know-how to recommend products and services that meet end user wants and needs.

Double-needle stitched: A finish used on a sleeve and/or bottom hem that uses two needles to create parallel rows of visible stitching, yielding a cleaner, more finished look and added durability.

Drop needle: A knit fabric characterized by vertical lines in the cloth. Created by "dropping" or eliminating one or more needles from the needle cylinder.

End user: An individual or organization that is the actual consumer of a promotional product. End users typically purchase promotional products with the help of distributors and may rely on distributors to guide them through the promotion and purchasing process.

Eye loupe: Magnification device that allows users to view artwork at 800 percent ($8\times$ magnification).

Font: The complete set of type in a single typeface, including characters, numbers and punctuation marks. Each font has a different look and feel.

Four-color process: The process of layering four colors (cyan, magenta, yellow, and black) to create full-color images and text.

Four over one or 4/1: The process of printing materials with a four-color (full color) process and one side and a single color—typically black—on the other.

Freemium: A gift given in advance of the purchase, theoretically "guilting" the recipient to act.

Garment washed: A process where softeners are added to finished garments to help cotton fibers relax or "bloom," resulting in a fabric with a thicker appearance, reduced shrinkage and softer hand.

Gigabyte: A billion bytes (or 1,000 megabytes) of data.

Graphic arts: A trade centered on the preparation of materials for print.

Halftone: A photograph that has been overlaid with a tone pattern composed of dots uniform in density but varying in size. Allows images to be printed with one pass in varying shades (e.g., white, gray and black).

Headline: A large, often bold caption at the beginning of an article or advertisement that summarizes the piece's premier message.

Herringbone: A chevron or zigzag pattern knit into fabric.

High-profile: A style of cap featuring a high slope and stiff fabric lining. Less fitted.

Houndstooth: A medium-size broken-check effect that is knit into the fabric.

Interlock knit: A fabric featuring two layers knit into one to form a thicker, heavier texture. Features a more natural stretch than jersey knit, soft and hand has the same appearance and feel on both sides.

Imprint area: The area where graphics may appear on any promotional product.

Imprint configuration: The position of graphic elements relative to one another. The two most common imprint configurations are logo on the left and logo on top.

Imprint orientation: The position of graphics relative to the product on which they are printed.

Jacquard knit: A pattern that is knit directly into the fabric generally featuring two or more colors.

Kerning: Spacing between letters.

Layout: Preliminary drawing or mockup of graphic design.

Leading: The amount of vertical space between lines of text. Measured in points. (Rhymes with heading.)

Logo: A symbol or illustration used as an identifying mark by a business.

Low-profile cap: A style of cap with a low slope that is more closely fitted to the head. Can be either structured or unstructured.

Media: Methods for delivering messages that include television, radio, print advertisements and promotional products.

Megabyte: 1,000 bytes of data.

Mercerized: A fabric that has gone through a process to produce a smooth, lustrous hand.

Mesh: Similar to pique knit but with a more open texture for increased breathability. Larger knit than cool weave.

Microfiber: Tightly woven fabric featuring a fine polyester thread. Has a suede-like finish and a luxurious, soft feel. Naturally water repellent and can be waterproof when specially treated.

Negative: The image obtained from the original in conventional photographic processes featuring reversed tones. Positive prints are generated from negatives.

One over one or 1/1: Both sides are printed with one color of ink.

Opaque: Not admitting light. Also can involve eliminating parts of images to prevent reproduction.

Overrun: Amounts of product or materials produced in excess of the ordered amount.

Pad printing: Printing process using rubber pads to imprint an image onto small areas or products.

Pica: A printing-industry unit of measure approximately equal to one-sixth of an inch. There are 12 points to each pica. Usually used to measure width of a column of text.

Pigment dyed: A process used to create a distressed or washed look.

Pima lisle: Fabrics created through a special manufacturing process that twists long strands of two-ply, 100 percent cotton fiber together, resulting in a lightweight, durable, and extremely soft fabric.

Pique knit: A type of fabric featuring a finely textured surface similar to a waffle-weave or bird's nest pattern.

Pixel: The smallest building block of a computerized graphic. The more pixels per inch, the higher the resolution and the sharper the image.

Placket: The part of the shirt or jacket where the panels fasten together.

PMS: Pantone Matching System. A universal printing reference for color, shades, and tones.

Point: A vertical measurement used in typesetting. One point equals one 72nd of an inch.

Popcorn pique: Alternating rows of two different knits.

Poplin: Tightly woven, durable, medium-weight cotton-blend fabric featuring a ribbed variation and slight ridge effect.

PostScript: The common graphic-description language developed by Adobe, Inc., that can define graphic shapes with mathematical formulas, allowing them to be precisely enlarged or reduced.

Premium: Promotional product given in response to an action.

Printing: Method used to transfer an image onto a material or product.

Print-ready artwork: Camera-ready or flight-ready art.

Promotional product: Any useful object that carries an imprint for the purpose of advertising a company, theme, individual, or concept.

Raglan sleeves: Sleeves set with a diagonal seam from the neck to the armpit.

Register: Correct positioning of art on an object.

Registration marks: Lines or symbols that appear on multicolor artwork to ensure proper alignment.

Resolution: Degree of sharpness that a computer display or printing device is capable of producing. The higher the resolution, the sharper the image.

Rib knit: A textured knit that has the appearance of vertical lines. It is highly elastic and is noted for its "memory."

Ring-spun yarn: Yarn made by continuously twisting and thinning a rope of cotton fibers to make the short hairs stand out, resulting in a stronger yearn with a soft hand.

Sandwashed: A process in which the fabric is washed with fine lava rocks or rubber or silicon balls, resulting in a softer fabric with a relaxed look and reduced shrinkage.

Scanner: A device that inputs an image into the computer. The higher the resolution of the scanner, the better the quality of the image.

Screen: A pattern of black dots that represents an intermediate tone between white and solid black.

Side vents: Slits found at the bottom of side seams. They are fashion details that allow for comfort and ease of movement.

Stonewashed: A process in which the fabric is washed with fine lava rocks or rubber or silicon balls, resulting in a softer fabric with a relaxed look and reduced shrinkage.

Straight type: Refers to an imprint that consists of text only, no logo.

Structured cap: A style of cap featuring a lined front consisting of buckram (a stiff fabric), which controls the slope of the cap.

Substrate: Any object that can accept an imprint.

Supplier: A manufacturer or master distributor that supplies promotional products sold through distributors and intended for end users.

Taped seams: A strip of fabric sewn to the seam of a garment to prevent distortion. Also may aid in waterproofing.

Tencel: A fabric made from the cellulose found in wood pulp that is processed into a delicate, silk-like fabric.

Text: An imprint comprised of letters.

Trade-show program: A professionally designed system that allows an exhibitor to maximize its return on investment utilizing promotional products as part of the marketing mix.

Twill: A fabric characterized by micro-diagonal ribs producing a soft, smooth finish.

Typeface: A specific version of a typestyle that has a clearly definable characteristic.

Typesetting: The process of using a computer to create text. Used to match available imprint space.

Underrun: The amount short of a complete order.

RESOURCE GUIDE

Charities
AIDS Research Alliance of America
www.aidsresearch.org
American Cancer Society
www.cancer.org
American Heart Association
www.amhrt.org
American Institute of Philanthropy
www.charitywatch.org
American Red Cross
www.redcross.org
Charity America
www.charityamerica.org
Habitat for Humanity
www.habitat.org
National Center for Charitable Statistics
www.nccs.urban.org
The United Way of America
www.unitedway.org

Demographic Data
Maponics
www.maponics.com
(800) 762-5158
United States Census Bureau
www.census.gov

Direct Mail
Impact Products, LLC

9171 Gazette Ave.
Chatsworth, CA 91311
Phone: (818) 280-0199
Fax: (818) 280-0239
www.impactproducts.net
United States Postal Service
(800) ASK-USPS® or (800) 275-8777
www.usps.com

Industry Information

Promotional Products Association International
3125 Skyway Circle North
Irving, Texas 75038-3526
(888) I-AM-PPAI (426-7724)
www.ppa.org

Public Relations

Public Relations Society of America
33 Maiden Lane, 11th Fl.
New York, NY 10038-5150
Phone: (212) 460-1400
Fax: (212) 995-0757
www.prsa.org

Trade Show Exhibits

Impact Products, LLC
9171 Gazette Ave.
Chatsworth, CA 91311
Phone: (818) 280-0199
Fax: (818) 280-0239
www.impactproducts.net

Discover How to Get More Information from the Author . . .

    Get an Additional $2,650 Worth of FREE Gifts from the Author
    Copy this page and FAX to (818) 280-0239
    Or go to www.thesilentsalesmen.com and use the password book-
offer to get:

1. Three months of the *Black Belt Marketing Newsletter.*
2. Three months of exclusive audio interviews with leading business experts.
3. Free access to Members Only web site.
4. Access to the Platinum Resource Directory.
5. Blogger Riches e-book Program.
6. Audio CD Interview with author and speaking expert Joel Bauer.
7. Audio CD Interview with author and persuasion expert Dave Lakhani.
8. Audio CD Interview with Psycho Psybernetics expert Matt Furey.
9. Audio CD Interview with offline and online publicity experts.
10. Audio CD Interview for 101 Pointers for trade show excellence.
11. Special Report: "How to Get In To See Anybody Anytime."
12. Attend FREE The Ultimate 2-Day Business Building Seminar ($1,995 Value) 2 Tickets Included.

    There is a one-time charge of $7 to cover postage for ALL three months of the *Black Belt Marketing* newsletter membership and audio CDs. You have no obligation to continue receiving the newsletter at the lowest price we offer ($49 per month United States and Canada and $54 per month International). You may cancel at any time.

Name _____
Address _____
City, State, Zip, Country _____
Phone and Fax _____
E-mail _____
Credit Card # _____
Expiration and Code _____
Signature _____
Date _____

INDEX